Bad Times, Good Friends

*The author (right) in front of the ruins on Kurfürstendamm in
Berlin, 1946—one year after the end of World War II.*

Bad Times, Good Friends

A PERSONAL MEMOIR

Ilse-Margret Vogel

Harcourt Brace Jovanovich, Publishers
San Diego   New York   London

The passage from "A Hunger Artist" on page 8 is from *The Penal Colony* by Franz Kafka.
Permission for its use was given by Schocken Books, Random House, Inc.

Library of Congress Cataloging-in-Publication Data
Vogel, Ilse Margret.
Bad times, good friends: a personal memoir/Ilse-Margret Vogel.
—1st ed.
p.   cm.
Summary: The author tells how she and some of her friends struggled
to survive and resist Nazi domination in Berlin from 1943 to 1945.
ISBN 0-15-205528-2
1. Vogel, Ilse Margret—Juvenile literature.   2. World War,
1939–1945—Germany—Berlin—Juvenile literature.   3. World War,
1939–1945—Personal narratives, German—Juvenile literature.
4. World War, 1939–1945—Underground movements—Germany—Berlin—
Juvenile literature.   5. Anti-Nazi movement—Germany—Berlin—
Juvenile literature.   6. Berlin (Germany)—History—Juvenile
literature.   7. Artists—Germany—Berlin—Biography—Juvenile
literature. [1. Vogel, Ilse Margret.   2. World War, 1939–1945—
Personal narratives, German.] I. Title.
D757.9.B4V64   1992
943.1'55086'092—dc20   91-43869
[B]

Designed by Camilla Filancia
Printed in the United States of America
First edition   A B C D E

To Nancy and Eric

For whom my love WILL-BLOOM

Forever

—I. M. V.

Contents

Foreword

ALL THESE STORIES take place in Berlin during the last two years of Nazi Germany, 1943–1945, up to the bitter end, when the Russian army fought in Berlin and conquered the city. I was approaching thirty during those years and so were most of my friends.

These stories are about our lives. We all hated Hitler, his ideology, his lies, his crimes, a regime without freedom, without humanism, and so blatantly without justice. We cannot boast great deeds. We did not assassinate or physically harm any Nazis, but we did frequently risk our lives resisting them by helping people who, for racial or political reasons, were being pursued and persecuted. We also gave shelter and assistance to those who, for moral or ethical reasons, were draft evaders. It may seem strange to readers that people, especially young men, could slip through the well-organized and well-applied net of government and military restrictions. It was strange, and it was mainly only possible in the big cities, where people could become lost among the crowds. Many Germans came to Berlin in order to *untertauchen*, dive underground. In a way, it became easier and easier for people to slip through Hitler's net as the war went on and bombardments increased and chaos reigned.

Nowadays, I am frequently asked: "Why didn't you leave Berlin, where you were in so much danger from the frequent bombardments?" The answer is that in smaller towns, though they were safer from bombardments, other very serious dangers existed. Anyone who did not follow the rules and regulations of the Nazis, and who did not appear to support Hitler, was easily spotted; once spotted, the concentration camps were not far behind. Neighbors were even instructed and rewarded for spying on one another. Only in big cities could a person get away with un-Nazi behavior. In Görlitz, my hometown, one became suspect—and could even be denounced and arrested—for not using the required Hitler greeting: raising the right arm and saying, "Heil Hitler."

When I went home for the holidays, it often happened that my mother, knowing I refused to utter this greeting, made me stand outside the store in which she wanted to shop—often in the bitter cold. She knew that I, entering the store, would have said, "Guten Tag," good day, which had been the customary greeting before the Hitler years.

The Nazi Party and its functionaries had a much stronger grip on the people who lived in the small towns, where the population as a whole was much easier to control and observe. I am certain that I, an impulsive person, would have ended up in a concentration camp if I had not moved to a large city. Among the Berliners, who were known for their resilience, their gallows humor, and their independence, a person like me was safer—in spite of the bombardments.

Some people may wonder why I never fled Germany entirely. This answer, too, is simple. My friends and I always believed the war would be over quickly, and Hitler would be defeated; there was no reason for us to flee our country. And as time passed, and bit by bit the city crumbled around us, we, as is human nature, became more accepting of the hardships placed upon us. We also realized that, in our own way, we were helping to resist the Nazis.

Nearly half a century has gone by, and since I am not a historian, nor did I take notes at the time, some dust has settled over the events, and some dates may be inaccurate. But what I am writing down did happen and is unforgettably etched in my mind.

If readers wonder why I, only now—nearly half a century later—am moved to write about those years, I can explain: Many of my American friends, especially Nancy Willard and Stanley Moss, who have heard me talk about the war years in Berlin, have urged me to write about them. I have finally given in, knowing that although there are many books and films about Hitler's terrible regime and the holocaust, most Americans have no knowledge of the hardships and dangers people like my friends and I had to face in everyday life. Even greater is my wish to make people aware of the fact that not all Germans were Nazis; there were some who, though not falling in the category of "heroes," were brave enough to risk their lives by their own special way of resisting. To write about all this, I simply needed the distance of time and more strength to relive these painful experiences.

Bad Times,
Good Friends

Ilse

B E F O R E I tell you about my friends and the years I spent in Berlin, I think you should know something about my life before those years.

Upside down, that is how I entered this world. My twin sister had made her entry the normal way: head first. She was already one hour old when the attending doctor, who had not been able to stop my mother's bleeding, wrung his hands and, despair in his voice, announced: "For heaven's sake! There's another one in there!"

At what stage I had decided to turn upside down nobody knows. Maybe it was a refusal on my part to leave the dark, warm quietude that had sheltered me for nine months.

I was neither expected nor welcomed. For my sister, a name—Erika—and a cradle were waiting. For me, nothing had been prepared, and I was put on Father's writing desk—just for one night. The following day, I was brought to a hospital because the doctor, pulling reluctant me out of my mother's womb, had broken one of my legs.

Later in life, when I was good at writing essays in school, my mother used to say: "Of course, you spent your first night in this world on a writing desk."

To me, however, in hours of unhappiness and despair, it seemed that the reception I got entering the world was proof that I should never have entered it at all.

My early childhood, I was told, was spent trying to hold my own against my livelier, stronger, and sometimes aggressive twin sister. She had mastered walking before I had, making her rounds in the crib by holding on to the railing. Barely able to stand on wobbly legs, all I could do was remain in one place, clinging to the railing. Of course, I was nothing but an obstacle for Erika, and each time she encountered me during her exuberant rounds in this little cage, I was knocked down. Screaming and pulling myself up again, I was ready for the next push over.

"Erika is so *rück-sichs-loss*"—a mispronunciation of the word for inconsiderate—I often lamented later, when language was given to me.

And it was language that enabled Erika to make clear to me that I had to take orders from her. She was older than I . . . a whole hour older! I partly disliked and partly admired her for her domineering spirit.

We grew up in Sybillenort, in a big house, surrounded by a large garden. These were the harsh years of World War I, but we, as children, did not feel anything of its deprivations. Our parents and grandmother took good care of us.

Erika and I were inseparable, tied together by frequent fights, games mostly invented by Erika, and hours of great tenderness. When Erika died from diphtheria, shortly before our ninth birthday, it was a great hurt to me, and it was not made easier by what Erika's death did to our mother: she had a nervous breakdown.

Young as I was, I could not understand. All I saw and felt was that Mother had changed so much. She spent most of her days in bed, in a darkened room, weeping. Seldom did she join us at mealtime and seldom did she speak to me.

One day she took me by the hand and pulled me into a dark

closet. "Smell this," she said, covering my face with something soft and, to my nose, scentless. "It's the shirt your sister died in," Mother explained, sobbing. I, too, began to cry and instantly was engulfed in a tight embrace that took my breath away.

What I did not know at the time, and learned only much later, was that Mother had found the glass vial that had contained the antidiphtheria serum with which the doctor had injected Erika. The date on it showed its usefulness had expired months before.

Life changed drastically. Now I was an only child and suffered from my mother's overprotection.

I remember not being allowed to go to school because the newspapers were full of gruesome reports about children who were abducted and killed; their bodies, ground up and mixed with beef (a rare commodity), were packed in tin cans and sold for human consumption. Besides, my mother would argue, in the nearby country school I would get lice. Well, I would have gladly put up with lice in exchange for the camaraderie of other children. There weren't any children my age in the neighborhood, and I often felt lonely.

An exemption that freed me from going to school was asked for and granted because my father had once been a teacher. By now he was in and out of jobs because of the hard times that followed World War I. Never, however, did he give me a single lesson. For four years, I was taught by my mother and grandmother.

When I was ten years old, we left Sybillenort and moved to the town of Görlitz, in Silesia, one of Germany's most eastern provinces. Here a new part of my life began. When I was in my teens, I attended the Latin School in Görlitz, where I founded strong and lasting friendships.

A certain childhood melancholy gave way to enjoyment and

gaiety, at least when I was not with my family. I tried to stay away from home as much as possible because the older I grew, the more I became aware that my parents' marriage was not made in heaven. Their frequent quarrels were followed by long periods during which they did not talk to each other. This pained me even more than their quarrels. I remember long Sunday walks with Father walking ten steps ahead of Mother while I, darting back and forth, tried in vain to start a conversation between them.

Further hardship was added due to the fact that Father, torn out of his profession as a schoolteacher, could never earn quite enough money to support us. Even with Grandmother, my mother's mother, helping out, there was a steady shortage of money, which, among other things, cut my school years short. Two years before the *Abitur*, the big examination which would have made me eligible to attend a university, I had to leave school. A painful decision because I loved school. I had been drawing and painting a lot and was considered talented. But now there was not the slightest hope that my dream of going to Berlin to study at the Art Academy could come true. Instead I took a course in typing and shorthand without being interested in either of them.

As I see it now, it was not surprising, then, that I gave in to the intensive courting of a friend of my father—only a few years younger than my father. And in the end, I married this man. The town of Görlitz was appalled: Dr. Vogel, the highly respected dental surgeon, had divorced his second wife in order to be free to pursue and marry me. But after a short, unfulfilled, and unhappy marriage, I left my husband, intending to start divorce proceedings. Twenty-four hours later he killed himself. My despair and guilt were overwhelming.

Now known as a "femme fatale" in Görlitz, I fled to Berlin, where a secretarial position had been arranged for me by a relative living there. Slowly, very slowly, I took hold of myself and began to enjoy life among the new friends I was making. We shared interests as well as anxieties and, very important during those years, a hatred for Hitler. The war had not broken out yet but was feared by those of us who had not fallen under Hitler's hypnotic and devastating spell.

And now begins my account of the years that followed: Harrowing years of bombardments, hunger, and fires, up to the conquest of the city of Berlin by the Russians. And, of course, of the friendships that helped me to endure and finally survive those years.

The Kleine König
The Little King

RUDOLPH KÖNIG was the skinniest man I had ever met in spite of an enormous appetite that could never be satisfied. His looks were in total contrast to what was "desirable" in Germany during the years of Hitler's Thousand Year Reich. He had a dark complexion, fat lips, and large eyes, the black iris floating in the bluish white of the eyeball. A long nose seemed to cut his face vertically into two different parts. One ear was larger than the other. Pitch-black hair hung in unwieldy strings over a narrow, high forehead. His small chin and cheeks were covered by a blackish blue film only a few hours after shaving.

Always he held his head at a slight angle over his narrow, drooping shoulders, from which a poorly fitted jacket hung loosely over what seemed to be a stick body. Not an ounce of fat on the whole figure. But his hands! Long and narrow with beautifully shaped fingernails, they were strangely pale in comparison to his facial darkness.

One of his hands clutched a walking cane the moment he left the shelter of a house and stepped into the street. His normal bouncy, quick gait changed into a limp. A young man in civilian clothing and looking so un-Aryan was in constant danger of being stopped by military controls trying to catch draft evaders or "undesirables." A heavy limp provided an obvious explanation for not being in uniform and offered protection against being stopped and questioned. Sometimes, however, when walking on a deserted street away from the center of town, König would abandon the limp. It was strenuous. Especially so because the fully stuffed briefcase in his cane-free hand was heavy, pulling down one shoulder even further, making the whole figure look lopsided and pitiable.

"You must meet Rudolph König," a friend of mine had insisted. "He will outdo even you in raging against Hitler. I've known him for several years and like him, though his existence is a mystery to me."

"A mystery?"

"Yes," said my friend. "It's a mystery how he manages to escape being drafted. Once he showed me a wrinkled piece of stationery—a Doktor Markes on the letterhead—in which he was diagnosed as suffering from a severe spinal deformity. My further questions König answered only with a smile and silence."

The *Kleine König*! That was how I thought of him, and sometimes called him so. He didn't mind. He took it as a sign of affection and tenderness, which it was.

What a presence he assumed in my life from the time he limped me home from the apartment of my friend to my small dwelling off the Kurfürstendamm!

Arriving in my room, König put down his briefcase with a sigh of relief. I went to the kitchen and brewed two cups of *real* coffee, a rare and precious treat.

" 'A Hunger Artist,' " König said, holding an open book in his hands when I returned to the room. "May I read you 'A Hunger Artist'?"

I put the coffee tray on the table beside the couch and sat down facing him. He had settled down in the only easy chair I owned. His cane leaned against the wall and his briefcase lay deflated on the floor, its contents, many books, strewn round his feet.

He took one hasty sip of coffee and immediately began to read. I was a bit startled. I did not know him well enough then to know there was no small talk within him. No conventional courtesy: "Thank you for the coffee," or "How nice your room is." He immediately came to the things that were important to him at that very moment. Right then it was "A Hunger Artist." Or was it his intention to find out my reaction to a writer he appreciated so much and I did not know at all? This, however, was a thought that occurred to me only weeks later, after we had become friends.

He read: " 'During these last decades the interest in professional fasting has markedly diminished. It used to pay very well to stage such great performances under one's own management, but today that is quite impossible. We live in a different world now. At one time the whole town took a lively interest in the hunger artist.' "

König put down the book. "It's by Kafka," he said. "Do you know Franz Kafka?"

"I don't," I said, but I wanted to, the words were so powerful. "Please, go on."

And König continued reading about the hunger artist, who for days and days sat inside a small, barred cage. He was surrounded by a group of onlookers, watching to make sure he would not take a single bite of food. Most of the time he was withdrawn, sitting with half-shut eyes. Once in a while he took a sip of water to moisten his lips. And when after forty days his impresario broke off this performance, the hunger artist wanted to go on. He felt he was in his best fasting form and felt cheated of the fame he would get by breaking his own record. There were no limits to his capacity for fasting, he felt, because it was easy for him. And besides, the mere thought of a meal, which was presented to him now, nauseated him.

When König finished reading Kafka's haunting tale, the spell was cast: Kafka got deep under my skin, in my head, and in my heart. I had listened attentively. As usual my stomach was empty. The hungry wolf inside it had growled for hours—little did I know at this first meeting with König that there were a dozen wolves howling inside his stomach. But Kafka had lifted me outside myself. The seeming ecstasy of his hunger artist transferred itself to me. My body and its needs did not seem to exist until the Kleine König had closed the book.

Silence.

"Good?" König asked.

I nodded eagerly. My cheeks were hot in the cool room. My stomach, an ever-present nuisance by its emptiness, growled, but did not really bother me. "Tell me about Kafka," I pleaded.

König did. And I knew a great joy lay ahead of me, reading more of the writings of this author.

"I have all of Kafka's books, among the thousands of books I own," König said. "Unfortunately, or thank goodness, most of them are already out of the city. In the home of my parents in the country. Less danger there to go up in flames."

"A pity," I said. "I'd like to read some of Kafka's books."

"Well," said König, "next week when I take another load of books out there, I'll bring some Kafkas back for you. All right?" Then, looking shyly at me, he asked, "Maybe you would like to come with me to the country?"

I nodded yes.

"It's a long and slow walk," he explained. "I have to pull a cart loaded with books and, of course, I must keep on limping. At least half of the ten-mile walk leads through the city and the suburbs."

"That's all right," I said. "I'm a good walker."

"After we leave the suburbs," König continued, "the country is beautiful. Open fields and lakes. No bombed-out houses any-more. And then . . ." He stopped for moment, and his face lit up. "And then Mother will have a meal for us. A *real* meal."

"All that sounds fine," I said. "Let me know when you go again. I'm looking forward to accompanying you. I can help pull the cart."

We said good-bye to each other, and König left.

A few minutes later the doorbell rang.

"Forgive me," the Kleine König muttered. "Could I stay half an hour longer? It's not quite dark yet. I feel better walking in the dark."

I let him in. He sat down in his chair again, folding his hands over his walking cane and resting his chin on them. His liquid eyes moved slowly around my room. "It's nice here," he said. After a while, he pointed to a painting of sunflowers and asked if I had painted it.

"Yes, I did. My homage to Van Gogh," I said, laughing.

"And that, over there, your homage to Nolde?"

I nodded.

"Nice," he said.

I felt a bit ashamed. "It's all so eclectic," I murmured. "I'm working and waiting to find my own style," I continued apolo-getically. "But as things are nowadays, it's hard to get canvas and paint. Especially when one doesn't belong to the Art Association of the Party. Also, peace of mind is hard to come by."

"I know, I know," König said, "and . . ."

I waited for him to finish the sentence, but he didn't. I saw he felt uneasy. Since I didn't know why, I kept silent, too.

A few moments later, casting his eyes to the floor, he asked, "Do you happen to have a slice of bread in the house? I can give you a coupon from my ration card."

"I have a few slices left, and I won't accept your coupon," I replied. But when I returned from the kitchen with two slices of bread, I saw his coupon on the small table beside the couch.

"I have a little jam my mother sent last week," I said. "It's not as good as she used to make before the war, but it does cover up the sawdust flavor of the bread. Please take some."

"No," he said. "Your mother made it for you."

I did not put any jam on my slice, either. Slowly I munched the dry, awful-tasting bread, but König ate fast and greedily. Then he fished in the pocket of his jacket and pulled out another coupon.

With a sheepish smile he asked, "Is it possible to have another slice?"

I was glad I had one more slice left. I fetched it from the kitchen and watched him devour it. A change came over him while he ate. His eyes were fixed on the slice of bread, which he hastily shoved into his mouth. Between bites, he did not lower the hand holding the bread. He kept it directly under his nose to rip off the next bite even before his mouth was empty. And it then dawned on me that there was more than one ravenous wolf inside König.

Once it was dark enough, I said good-bye to him at the door and secretly stuffed the two bread coupons he had left on my table into the pocket of his jacket.

König's "Hunger Artist"—that was the way I thought about the Kafka story König had read to me—stayed in my mind and didn't give me any peace. I decided to go to a bookstore, hoping to find another of Kafka's books. I was glad the store where I usually bought my books was still intact, although most of the houses close to it were in ruins. I was disappointed, however, not to see the owner, Fräulein Spaeth, a nice, elderly lady with whom I usually enjoyed a short but interesting chat.

"She left her store in my charge," said the young lady in the store when I asked for Fräulein Spaeth. "She couldn't take the bombardments anymore and left for Bavaria. Can I help you?"

"I'm looking for books by Kafka," I replied. "Do you have any?"

"Kafka?" the young woman said with a frown, disgust in her voice. "I don't think so."

"Maybe there are some in the basement." The moment these words were out of my mouth I was horrified by my carelessness.

"How could they be in the basement?" the woman said, irritated. "Kafka is on the list of forbidden authors. His books were burned together with thousands of others shortly after Hitler came to power and cleansed Germany of the demoralizing influence of Jewish literature. The big book burning. Don't you remember?"

"Indeed I do," I said and turned my back to her. How I missed Fräulein Spaeth, who would go down to the basement to get rare and "forbidden" books for me. All the Faulkners, Thornton Wilders, and Hemingways I owned I had bought from her. Now, looking round the store, I saw a large Hitler portrait above the cash register. Then a pile of tiles astonished me. *Tiles?* I thought. In a bookstore?

"These are very good sellers," the young lady informed me, noticing my apparent interest. "Just read the clever and humorous messages."

And I did. Don't Fuss, Mensch! was written in decorative letters on the first one. Each Pot Finds a Fitting Lid, read the next. More and more of these fatuous slogans were made permanent on these tiles, and they were not inexpensive, either.

"From where do you get them?" I asked the young lady, who had not left my side.

With pride in her voice, she told me that a talented artist friend had painted them to her order. The Hitler portrait over the cash register was also his work. "If you buy more than twelve tiles, I can reduce the price," she informed me.

I shook my head. With anger I remembered that a few weeks before, my landlady had tried to buy some plain tiles to replace several damaged ones in her bathroom. Not available, she was told. The production of tiles, a commodity not belonging to the war effort, had ceased long ago.

There were also hideous postcards in the store. One showed a photomontage of Hitler and Churchill, side by side, Hitler grinning, Churchill frowning. I left the store, but a minute later I returned and bought one of the tiles. It read, Chin Up—It Can't Get Worse. I hoped it would amuse and appall my landlady.

A few days later König phoned, and we set a date for the book transport to the country. I looked forward to the walk toward Kafka and a mother-made meal. The three slices of bread I had shared with König had been my last ones for the week—no coupons left. I managed to borrow two slices from my landlady, and I still had one hundred grams of barley in the cupboard, which I boiled in salted and peppered water. My fat ration for the week was long gone. One apple was left, a big, beautiful one, but I intended to paint it before eating it.

Therefore the *real* meal loomed large on the horizon when König knocked on my door at eight o'clock on a Monday morning.

It was one of those unusually warm October days—so warm I wore a light cotton dress.

I opened the door and, seeing König, burst out laughing. "Are you going skiing?"

He looked bewildered when I gave a tug to the heavy, red woolen muffler around his neck, hanging down to his knees on both sides. Then he smiled. "I'm always cold. Forgive me."

He had left his little four-wheel handcart in the courtyard that separated the main house, fronting the street, from the so-called garden house lying behind it, where I lived. It was a stone-covered courtyard, not at all a garden, but here, in the fashionable section of Berlin, these houses were not called *Hinterhaus*, as in the poorer parts of the city, but *Gartenhaus*.

The cart's wheels rattled over the stony ground when we left, and several windows opened. Women peeked out, and I could imagine their thoughts: what a weird new admirer the girl from the ground floor has.

I knew I was a strange bird to them to start with. A suspicious one, too. In their minds, I had come from nowhere to share the much-coveted Gartenhaus apartment on the ground floor. A half-Jewish lady held the lease, and many of the occupants of the other apartments were waiting for the moment when this "undesirable" lady would be expelled. Many hoped to lay their hands on this very nice apartment. There was also a new law forbidding a single person to inhabit a four-room apartment. With each bombardment, more houses were destroyed and apartments became more scarce. So Frau Lasker had to take in a tenant: me. I occupied one room with bath and had the use of the kitchen. It also must have puzzled the other inhabitants of the house never to see me in the air-raid shelter. I simply did not go down when the sirens rang, choosing to disobey the law that ordered us to take shelter.

I couldn't stand the hysteria and talk in these places: *Well, this won't last much longer. Our Führer is successful on all fronts.* And so forth.

But this morning I was not bothered by what they might think. I was in a splendid mood. And König, whom I had known so far only as a very serious young man, was full of smiles and happy chatter.

When we were out on the street, I helped pull the cart, on which a high pile of books was secured by a crisscross of ropes.

"A nice street you're living on," König said. "In the center of town, and yet the street is lined with linden trees."

"Yes," I said, "it's heavenly when they are in bloom."

"The blossoms are valuable now. They make a good tea."

"Yes," I said, "but that isn't so important. It's the scent I love."

"Forgive me," König said.

"What for?" I asked.

"Oh, for being so materialistic." And he added in a murmur, "So food conscious."

It was only a short distance from my house in the Meineke-strasse to the Kurfürstendamm, where we turned right toward the truncated Gedächtniskirche, the Kaiser-Wilhelm Memorial Church. An awful sight. I averted my gaze. We walked along Budapester Strasse, which was now a row of demolished houses, most of them only roofless shells. Some, not completely destroyed, loomed behind mountains of rubble, neatly stacked up to the windows of the first floor. And the Zoologischer Garten, the zoological garden, that stood opposite these houses, with its splintered tree trunks was likewise a sad sight. I tried to behave as if I didn't see any of it.

Furtively, I looked at König and saw that he was well aware

of the horrible devastation. But, just like me, he obviously did not want to let the sight of it change the good mood we were in at the start of our long walk. However, when our eyes met for a second, König quickly turned his head and, motioning toward the splintered trees, he said, "Forgive me."

"Forgive you for what?"

"For leading you past all this."

"It's not your fault," I said. "How can you help it?"

He didn't answer. He shrugged, leaned forward, and quickened his pace. He looked helpless and vulnerable.

We went on walking until we reached Lützow Platz. Once it had been a large square of fine houses, with a park in its center where huge beautiful old trees rose from a well-kept green lawn. I couldn't trust my eyes: now there were no trees left. Instead of the beauty I remembered, there rose a sizable hill in the middle of what had been the lawn and where a fountain once had splashed. It took me several moments to realize that the rubble of the destroyed houses surrounding the park had been shoved to the middle of the place to clear the sidewalks. On a house still intact was one of the vicious posters one saw throughout the city. It showed the usual caricature of a Jew, a large-nosed man chasing a pretty blond girl. The caption read, The Jews Are Our Curse.

We had to stop in front of this poster to let a column of marching Hitler Youth pass by. Instinctively König turned his head away from the column and faced the poster. After a while, he nudged my elbow and said, "Doesn't he look a bit like me?" It gave me a start when he broke into a forced laugh.

"But, König," I said, "you don't look like that at all." And then, with anger in my voice, I added, "And Jews don't look like that, either. The whole poster is a lie. How can you say such a stupid thing?"

"Forgive me," König said. "Please, forgive me."

He did not turn toward the street again until he was sure the brownshirts had passed.

We started to walk again. After we crossed the Landwehrkanal, which in earlier years had carried many barges through Berlin, I was no longer familiar with the network of streets. But König knew them well. He had traveled them many times, he told me. It took us a half hour before we reached the suburbs and another hour to leave them behind.

In the suburbs, the air lost the gritty dustiness caused by the ruins. Only a few houses had been damaged by bombs.

Soon we were walking in the flat openness of potato fields, through meadows sprinkled with daisies and asters and colorful late-blooming stragglers, and, once in a while, a pine grove with its sharply scented needles. Walking became sheer joy. We didn't talk much. We walked briskly, at times smiling at each other.

"I can't believe it," exclaimed König, pointing to a church steeple not far away. "I can't believe we are nearly home already." He checked his wristwatch. "With your help it took half an hour less than it usually takes me to get to this spot. Are you sure we aren't walking too fast? Isn't it too strenuous for you?"

I assured him I was fine and enjoying myself.

"You must be hungry now?" he asked.

"Well . . . not much . . . well, yes, a bit, I guess."

"I am *terribly hungry*," he said, and the way he said it convinced me it was true.

König's mother must have seen us coming. She stood in front of her modest little house and greeted us warmly. I was startled by her looks: was this blond, plump, and buxom woman really the mother of the dark, skinny, books-and-food-devouring young man I knew?

"The meal is ready," she said, ushering us immediately into the dining room. The table was loaded with so many serving dishes that I expected more members of the family to join us. But only three plates were laid out, and Frau König said, "It's just the three of us. My husband and my daughter are at work."

Amazed, I looked at the variety of food: The pretty orange baby carrots were generously sprinkled with deep green parsley. The green string beans glistened in a light buttery sauce. Dill and chives topped the large bowl of white cabbage, and the red cabbage, Frau König told us, had been simmered in a bit of red wine and apples. Another large plate was heaped with boiled potatoes under a green veil of fresh dill.

There was also a plate of meat, but not too much of it. Apologetically, Frau König said, "Meat, I can't grow, unfortunately." And she added, "It's supposed to be beef."

"What do you mean by 'supposed to'?" Rudolph wanted to know.

"Well," she said, "nowadays one can't be sure."

"Do you want to suggest it could be horse meat, Mother?" asked Rudolph.

"Not impossible, but don't let us think about that now. Let's enjoy it." She looked at me inquiringly.

"So what?" I said. "Germans don't like horse meat, but the French love eating it. It's sold in many fine specialty stores in France."

There were two thin slices of meat for each of us. Frau König, however, ate only one and slid her second slice onto her son's plate.

"Let me give you a slice, too," I said to the Kleine König, and I think he would have accepted it if Mother König had not intervened.

"For Mother," König said, "who loves flowers passionately, it was a real sacrifice to transform her flower garden into a vegetable garden."

"Yes, yes," said Mother König with a little sigh as she put more carrots and green beans on my plate. "But it happened only gradually. It started with just two tomato plants in the flower bed. The red fruit looked pretty among the yellow marigolds and purple cosmos. The following year the gladioli had to make room for the green beans, and the cucumbers needed lots of space and squeezed out my dahlias. Well . . . and so on and on until just a few zinnias are now left among the many vegetables."

Soon she and I stopped eating. The meat and the vegetables were gone. A few potatoes were left, and Rudolph still had what Mother König called "a hungry look" on his face.

"Rudolph, my child," she said and, shaking her head, she put two more potatoes on his plate. "He always was a heavy eater," she said, turning to me.

I nodded and smiled.

Getting up from the table, the Kleine König grabbed the last potato and, chewing it, said, "I have to unload my books now."

"I'll help," I said and thanked Frau König for the meal, then followed Rudolph out to the book cart.

It wasn't easy to climb the narrow, steep stair to the attic with an armload of heavy books. Hundreds of books were already stored there in rows and rows on simple wooden shelves. Only a few shelves were still empty.

"I'm afraid," said the Kleine König, "this attic will not hold all my books. There are still many more in the city."

We emptied the little cart and were ready to leave when Rudolph remembered Kafka. He quickly located the Kafka books on the alphabetically arranged shelves. His hand glided back and forth over the backs of the books until he pulled out one of them. "*The Castle*," he said. "Maybe you should read this one first. I hope you'll enjoy it . . . though it isn't really joyful reading. But . . . I love it."

Mother König put a large jar of mixed vegetables in Rudolph's hand and a smaller one in mine before we departed.

"Come back soon," she said, shaking my hand.

"I wish she would," said the Kleine König, looking searchingly into my face.

The walk back to town with the empty cart seemed easy. We walked quickly, singing at times. Suddenly, a large shepherd dog came running toward us, and König stopped walking. His head turned rapidly in all directions as if searching for something.

"What is it?" I asked.

"Oh . . . nothing," he said meekly, but fear spread over his face.

The dog quickened his pace and, wagging his tail, came very close to us. König let go of the handle of the cart and stepped behind me.

"König," I said, "the dog means no harm. He's wagging his tail, greeting us in a friendly way."

"I don't know," König said. "I don't trust dogs. One once bit me when I was a child."

By now the dog had stopped in front of me and, jumping up, put his front paws on my chest, trying to lick my face. I told König this was a friendly gesture. I had grown up with a big shepherd, I told him, and I knew how to handle the situation. But König, obviously in fear and seeking protection, pressed himself against my back. I patted the exuberant animal and told him he was a good dog. And even before I tried to get rid of him, a shrill whistle coming from a nearby birch grove instantly made the dog turn his back and run away.

König heaved a sigh of relief and thanked me. "You'll probably laugh at me," he said.

"No, I won't. Not at all."

The truth was I was somehow moved by what had happened. Even proud in a way. I, who was often afraid of things, sometimes of ridiculous and irrational things, I, for once, had been the strong one. Someone a friend could lean on. It was obvious, however, that König felt ashamed.

"A grown man shouldn't be afraid of a dog," he said. In a faint voice he added, "Or of bombardments. But . . . I am. Forgive me."

"Nothing to forgive," I said. "Many people are afraid of bombardments. Come to think of it, all my friends are. They all hurry to the shelter when the sirens sound. And I, well, I'm afraid, too—in a way. I'm afraid of spending so many hours in the shelter with all those hysterical people, most of them Hitler admirers. Besides, I'm a fatalist. I believe my life will end when it has to."

"Lucky you," Rudolph said.

"If you knew," I continued, "about my many silly fears, you would laugh at me."

König was tactful. He didn't ask what my fears were, and I was thankful.

We had walked for quite some time when I decided to tell him about one of my fears, hoping it might alleviate his feeling of shame. "Now, don't you think it's ridiculous that a grown-up girl like me kneels down at her couch every night before going to bed to check whether some *thing*, not *somebody*, mind you, might be hiding there? Some thing unimaginable. Maybe an arm. Just an arm, disembodied. Or a claw perhaps. A claw reaching out from under the couch when I am asleep, ready to drag me God knows where? You must admit, König, that that is worse than being afraid of a dog."

Rudolph had listened attentively. All he said, after I had finished, was, "Dear Ilse." And for a fraction of a second he put his hand on mine.

We had reached the suburbs when the air-raid sirens sounded.

"Oh, my God," said the Kleine König. "What shall we do?"

"Nothing," I said. "No bombs will fall here. We'll just keep on walking."

"No, I can't." His hand, lying close to mine on the handle of the cart, began to shake violently.

"König, what is it?"

"I'm afraid of the bombardments. Deathly afraid. We have to take shelter."

"But where?" I asked.

"Any damn house we pass."

"You really want to be in a shelter here? In a shelter probably filled with Hitler-loving Nazis?"

"It can't be helped." He let go of the handle of the cart and ran toward a large villa. "Forgive me," he called back over his shoulder, and by now his voice was trembling, too. He disappeared behind a gate.

I pulled the cart close to the fence surrounding the villa and prepared for a long wait. I could hear forbidding sounds, crashes and the incessant rumbling of flak coming from the city. But nothing happened close to where I was. After half an hour, the all clear sounded. König rejoined me instantly.

"Was it very fierce out here?" he asked, but before I could answer, he added, "How courageous you are. I admire you."

Thinking of the fear-ridden, trembling König, I shook my head and said, "Not to be afraid is nothing to be proud of. It's just something to be grateful for."

König seemed baffled. Still trembling, he said, "I'm cold." And, shivering, he wound his red woolen scarf tightly around his neck.

We walked quietly for quite some time before I asked König whether the house he lived in had a good air-raid shelter.

"No, it hasn't," he said. "Besides, like you, I do not want to be down there together with the other occupants of my house."

"What then do you do?" I asked.

"I have to go to a public shelter."

"Is one nearby?"

"Not really. It takes me about ten minutes, running fast, to reach the tunnel of the subway station."

"But then you lose a lot of time, having to get dressed and all. Don't you?"

König didn't answer.

I didn't know it then, but much later, when he felt closer to me, he confided that he never, never ever, got out of his clothes, which explained the strong scent of a strange eau-de-Cologne that always emanated from him. It had startled me the first time we met.

By now dusk had come. With horror we saw that the moonless sky over the inner city was not turning dark, but instead was tinged with streaks of red and dusty yellow. As we got closer to town, the smoke-filled air burned our eyes and made us cough. Fire engines, their sirens shrieking, rushed past us. The frantic shouting of people mingled with the belated explosions of bombs that had failed to go off when they first hit the ground. The noise became so unbearable that we stopped.

"Move on!" a harsh voice ordered. We did, but were turned back after a few steps. "This street is full of unexploded bombs," an air-raid warden told us. We turned back again, and through smoke and showers of sparks we slowly got away from the eastern sector, which had been so heavily hit during the raid.

Since it was dark by now, and the streets we were forced to take did not lie along König's usual route, we got lost frequently. Time and again we had to protect our faces from ashes and floating cinders in the air.

It took a long time to reach the west of Berlin where I lived, and once more, before we reached Meinekestrasse, König had to endure another scare.

On a rather deserted street, an S.S. man in his black uniform called, "Wait a minute!" He began crossing the street toward us.

König immediately bent down in order to hide his face and busied himself with one of the cart's wheels. But all the S.S. man wanted was to know the time.

"Half past seven," I said quickly, and he hurried off.

Finally arriving at my apartment, König asked whether he could come in for a little rest. Once inside, he opened the tall jar his mother had given him, sniffed it, and declared it to be a fine stew.

"Shall we eat it cold or would you like to warm it up?" he asked.

"Do you really want to eat it already?" I asked.

"Of course."

"I'll warm it up," I said. "All of it?"

"Certainly. I'm hungry after the long walk."

I heated the thick, delicious-smelling stew in the kitchen and brought it to König in a big bowl. His whole self was given to the act of eating; only once did he raise his eyes from the bowl before he emptied it. There was an animal-like childishness about him while he ate, and only after he finished did he become a civilized young man again. A satisfied smile spread over his face.

"How I envy Kafka's hunger artist," he said. "For him, starving is a joyous state of being."

After eating and now feeling rested, König got up to leave. I wanted to give him the jar his mother had given me, but he sternly refused to accept it.

"Will you come with me again next week?" he asked meekly.

I told him I would.

The following week, however, he could not go. And the week after, I had a cold I couldn't shake for several weeks. Then winter was upon us, and the daily struggle for the necessities of life got harder as the bombardments increased. Standing in line at the many different shops where I had to buy my meager food rations became more and more unpleasant. During the early war years most people had been civil, even friendly, while waiting. They had talked to one another about their hopes and fears. By now, however, people were at their nerves' end. Their sleeping hours were drastically reduced by the nearly nightly air-raid alarms. The law required every house to have an air-raid shelter and the law—if not fear—forced people to take shelter. But many people did not feel safe in these sometimes makeshift basement shelters. So they went to the huge public bunkers which, already at the beginning of the war, had been erected throughout the city.

One of these monstrous shelters, with its thick concrete walls, was near the Zoo railroad station, not more than a five- to ten-minute walk from where I lived. I had never been there but was astonished to learn that it was filled to capacity every night. Even before the alarm signal was sounded, thousands of people went there regularly to spend the night on bunk beds or on the floor. Many people still held war-essential jobs and had to get up early in the morning, and they were exhausted and short-tempered when they had to stand in line.

Though no book transports were planned during these winter months, König dropped in frequently, and he always had something to tell that was a challenge. His knowledge of literature was enormous. Music and art interested him also beyond the level of the average educated person. It was a pleasure to listen to him; it extended my life and mind. Politics we seldom discussed. We knew each other's opinions about the Nazis so well that talking about them seemed unnecessary to us. We chose other subjects that would cheer us up and lift us temporarily out of the daily miseries. Sometimes, however, such contrived and unbelievably stupid Wehrmacht communiqués came over the radio that we had to acknowledge them.

"Did you hear," König asked me one day, interrupting himself with a bitter laugh. "Did you hear that today our troops on the eastern front victoriously withdrew from the enemy? *Victoriously!*"

"You're joking," I said.

"No, no," König said. "This good news came over the Deutsch-landsender at noon. It came after the fanfare that always precedes reports of military victory."

"Ah," I said, "our propaganda minister has enriched the German language and coined a new phrase: victorious withdrawal."

König laughed again, but I couldn't. A strange man, I thought, and at that moment I realized how little I knew about König's daily life. Though we had become close friends, I didn't know where he lived nor how he supported himself. He hardly ever talked about himself. Not that he was evasive, nor I incurious. The situation just never led to my asking many questions. And he, not given to small talk, would always launch into conversation about one thing or another that was important and interesting to him at that very moment. I enjoyed his company and accepted him the way he was.

One day I had just returned from standing for hours in a long line at the bakery when König phoned, something he seldom did. He had told me once that he had an aversion to telephones, which I understood. I also did not like to talk to people without facing them; I felt it made lying so easy.

"Ilse," König said without any ado, "would you help me commit a crime? An honorable crime?"

I had to laugh. "A crime? What do you mean?"

"I'll tell you when I see you. You'll enjoy it. Trust me . . . just once."

"All right," I said, "I will."

"If there is no air raid, expect me tonight around ten o'clock, all right?"

"So late?"

"Yes, we can't act before midnight."

"All right, then," I said. "Come."

What a mystery! In my mind, crime, honorable or not, and König had no common denominator. I spent the whole afternoon wondering and guessing—König was certainly not the sort to do anything drastic or rash. He, for obvious reasons, wanted to be as inconspicuous as possible.

I was in a state of nervous excitement when shortly after ten König arrived.

"Tell!" I urged, hardly giving him time to sit down.

"Ilse," he began, "two fine artists need our help."

"Who are they?"

"Georg Kolbe and Busoni."

"I know who Kolbe is, a very fine sculptor. But Busoni? I've never heard of him."

"Busoni is likewise a fine artist, a composer—an Italian who lived in Berlin."

"I will be glad to help if they are in any kind of trouble. But König, don't such famous men have more important, I mean more influential friends than you and me? What can we do for them?"

"Well," König said, "as things are, it is just we who can do something. I have already appealed to another source, the Magistrate's Office of Berlin, and asked for help. But none is forthcoming. My urgent pleas weren't even acknowledged." König looked searchingly at me before he went on. "I hope you'll not be too appalled by my plan. You see, we'll have to go to the cemetery."

"The cemetery?" I thought I had misunderstood.

"Yes, the cemetery. You see, Busoni is dead, and he's buried in the Schöneberg graveyard. I used to visit his grave and enjoy the beautiful gravestone Kolbe had made for him. I was there again a couple of weeks ago. The whole cemetery was an awful sight— a battlefield it seemed. Most of the gravestones were lying flat on the ground, shattered. Others stood lopsided and cracked. The trees that made the graveyard seem like a park were uprooted, splintered, and lying crisscross over graves and headstones. It took me quite some time to locate Busoni's grave. Can you understand my sadness, Ilse, when I found the beautiful Kolbe angel tipped over, its face buried in the dirt and part of one wing chipped off? A tree trunk lay across the fallen angel. With great effort I succeeded in pulling the tree trunk away, and with my bare hands I shoveled a lot of dirt off the sculpture, hoping to upright it again. But . . . I couldn't."

König sighed and leaned back in his chair. He seemed as exhausted as if he had just now performed this arduous task.

"Poor König," I said. "Poor Kolbe. And poor Busoni, too. And now," I asked, "what can we do?"

"We have to rescue the angel, Ilse. That's what."

"You mean *steal* the angel? From the cemetery?"

"It's not exactly like stealing. You see, after I discovered what had happened to the angel, I immediately brought it to the attention of the cemetery administration, making them aware that a cultural monument had been damaged."

"And did they give you permission to remove the stone?"

"No, they didn't. They didn't react in any way. Not even after I wrote a second and a third letter. I finally went to the office and repeated what I had written to a clerk working there. He listened with a stony, bored face. 'If you knew, dear sir,' he said after I had finished, 'if you knew of the extremely urgent problems we have to solve daily, you would not bother us with trivia like this. Your report, however, will be filed, and after victory, we will see what we can do about it.' He rose, raised his arm, said, 'Heil Hitler,' and smiling at me with obvious dislike, he gestured toward the door."

König's eyes were fixed on my face, waiting for my response.

"A monster," I said furiously.

"Well, then," König said, "let's go."

"Where to?"

"The cemetery, of course. It's a dark, moonless night. The streets are deserted. We'll bring the angel back to your room."

"Let's just pray there won't be an air raid," I said as we both stood up.

It was a fifteen-minute walk to the cemetery. König found the fallen angel without difficulty. He didn't even use the flashlight he had brought along. We tried to upright the sculpture and carry it, but it was too heavy.

"We'll have to drag it," König said. "We can get a good grip on it under the spread wings."

And that's what we did; it worked rather well. After we left the cemetery, our precious burden glided easily on the concrete sidewalks. I hadn't seen the angel yet because it was too dark, but I was very curious. When we stopped for a rest, I ran my fingers over the angel's face. It didn't tell me much.

We reached Meinekestrasse, and at the entrance to my house a shaft of light fell on the pavement from an inefficiently blacked-out window. I saw something awful.

"Look, König!"

"Oh, my God," he said when he saw the distinct white streak our angel had engraved on the pavement.

Hastily we went inside and propped the sculpture up in a corner of my room, where full light fell on it. We did not talk. We just sat and looked and looked. Now I could marvel at its beauty.

"It's yours now, Ilse," König said.

I shook my head.

"For the time being at least," König said. "For the time being it is blessing your room."

"Thank you," I said, smiling. "Do you think we can do anything about the telltale streak in the street? It will lead from the cemetery directly to my house."

"No," he said. "Why should we? If the people responsible for taking care of damage to the cemetery should ever get interested in the disappearance of the gravestone, so much the better. Let them find their way here. We will explain and gladly turn the sculpture over if they provide the necessary care for it."

"All right," I said with a sigh of relief. "This thought will appease my conscience and let me sleep peacefully at night."

I hadn't seen König for a fortnight when one day I answered a knock at my door. By now the doorbell worked only a few hours a day when my block was allocated electricity. I opened the door and there stood the Kleine König, beside him a large dog.

Thinking the animal had joined König that very second and knowing his fear of dogs, I said, "Quickly, quickly," while trying to pull König inside and shut the door behind him.

But it didn't work. König held the dog on a leash.

"König!" I exclaimed in utter astonishment. "König!"

He smiled, patted the dog, and gently guided it inside. Words failed me, and König did not stop smiling. I shut the door.

"I'll explain," he said. He took off the leash and sat down. The dog sat beside him, nestling his head in König's lap.

"Tell me," I urged.

And König began: "A week ago I was riding home on the very last subway train. You know, they stop running early these days. It was around midnight and there were only a few people on the train. I got off at the end station, walked through the turnstile, handing my used ticket to the clerk, and was limping up the stairs when the clerk called after me, 'Hey, Mister! Your dog!' 'I have no dog,' I replied, but looking back I saw a large shepherd, taking its time, trudging up the stairs behind me. 'Take the beast with you,' the clerk ordered. 'It isn't my dog,' I said. 'It must belong to another passenger.' 'You were the only one leaving the train,' the clerk told me. 'Just the same,' I said, 'it's not my dog. I hate dogs!' 'Yes, yes, I know. Now you hate the poor dog and want to get rid of him. I know people like you. Not enough food for both of you. You'd rather eat the dog food yourself, hey?' He laughed an ugly laugh. I didn't answer, I just walked away."

"And the dog?" I asked.

"I didn't pay any attention to the dog. Out in the street it was pitch-dark. I couldn't see anything but a few stars in the sky above me. After a few minutes, however, I *heard* something, the thud of four feet—four paws, that is. I walked faster, even ran, but the thudding paws came closer. I heard breathing close to me, and then I felt a warm tongue licking my cold hand. I tried to shoo the dog away. I even stopped walking and talked to the dog the way I had heard you talk to a dog once. But the dog wouldn't leave, and he stayed at my side when I resumed walking. It's a ten-minute walk from the subway station to where I live, and I hoped to get rid of the dog before reaching home. Strangely enough, though I was annoyed by the dog, I wasn't really frightened."

"Good," I interjected.

"Arriving at my door, I told the dog I was sorry, but he couldn't come in. 'Good night, dog,' I said. 'Go now!' Not harshly, just firmly. I went inside and, being tired, I went to bed. But sleep would not come as easily as it usually does. Every few minutes I held my breath and listened, hoping to hear the dog walk away. I heard nothing. Then, when I was close to sleep, I heard scratching at my door. Light at first, but increasing as the minutes passed. I had to do something. I had to be tough and really shove the dog away, so I got up and opened the door."

König stopped talking, bent down to the dog's head still resting in his lap, and kissed it. I watched and waited.

"Well," he went on, "I was not prepared nor was I steeled for what happened next. The dog sat up on his hind legs and looked straight into my eyes. His beautiful green eyes sparkled in the shaft of light falling through the slit of my partially opened door. Ilse," and here König's voice trembled lightly, "Ilse . . . never has a living creature looked at me so pleadingly and . . . so lovingly."

"So you took him in," I said. "And now you are living happily ever after."

König nodded. "You have no idea, Ilse, how good it feels to have a warm, furry creature sleeping beside you. Of course, there is the problem of food. But somehow I must manage, even if I have to steal. First, however, I'll turn to Mother for help."

"Well," I said, "dogs aren't exactly vegetarians. But if you would let him run free in the country, he'll catch himself a rabbit or a mole."

"Let him run free?" asked König, shaking his head vehemently. "What if he doesn't come back?"

"I know," I said, "it would break your heart."

The dog, who had been sleeping for the last few minutes, woke up, shook himself, got up, and crossed the room to put one paw on my knee.

"He loves you, too," König said, fatherly pride in his voice.

And I began to understand. König was a very shy and private person. He didn't seem to have friends or a sweetheart. I even remembered him saying once, *Who could love an ugly man like me?* He lived alone and withdrawn. He had, however, a kingdom all his own: his books. And sharing what he read with someone like me seemed to be the only, the highest form of communication for him.

His sudden show of affection for the dog touched me deeply. At the same time, it worried me. The dog would complicate König's life tremendously. The food problem was obvious, but there was also the problem with König's way of walking. How could he manage to hold the walking stick, the leash, and carry the book-filled briefcase, which was as much a part of him as his arms and legs? And what of the air-raid shelters? No animals were allowed! I did not want to dishearten König and kept these thoughts to myself.

Meanwhile, the dog returned to König, who had taken a sheet of paper from his briefcase. "Listen to this, a speech by Winston Churchill."

"By Churchill?" I asked, astonished. "How did you get it?"

"An earlier teacher of mine, now living in Switzerland, some-times smuggles interesting material of this sort to me. This was Churchill's first speech after he became prime minister in May 1940. Do you want to hear it, Ilse?"

I eagerly nodded yes. And König read me the stirring speech in which Churchill assured his countrymen they would be victorious in the end. However, he did not shy away from adding that for the moment, he had nothing to offer but blood, toil, tears, and sweat.

I shuddered at the idea.

"A great statesman," König said.

I nodded, saying yes, but didn't know what more to say. I hadn't really grasped all of the speech and was going to ask König to read it once more when the air-raid sirens wailed.

Instantly König jumped up. "The dog," he said. "What to do with Rolf? They won't let me in the bunker with the dog."

"Of course not," I said. "I'll keep him here."

König hurried off.

I made the dog sit beside me on the couch. It was a heavy attack. Several bombs crashed nearby, and the doors and windows rattled in their frames. I was quite inured to that kind of thing, but the poor dog let out ear-shattering howls.

An hour passed before König returned, breathless and pale. "Just two houses away from your house, two houses are completely destroyed. There's a large crater in front of them now."

"Shall we go and see if we can help?" I asked.

"I don't think we can. Fire engines are there already, and the area is cordoned off. I'm happy you and Rolf are all right."

König hugged his dog, and I, happy to be alive, impulsively hugged the Kleine König, too. He was surprised. And so was I.

"Go home now," I said. "But if you don't mind, leave the Churchill speech with me, will you? I'd like to read it again."

"I will leave it for a few days, but you can't let it lie around in the open. Where will you hide it?"

"Don't worry, Churchill will keep Charlie Chaplin company under my bed."

Puzzled, König looked at me. "Chaplin?" he asked. "Under your bed?"

"Yes," I laughed. "I guess I never told you that a friend of mine, who once was an assistant to a German filmmaker, got hold of a print of Chaplin's latest picture, *The Great Dictator*. Of course, cinemas in Nazi Germany can't show it because the hero is the spitting image of our Führer. But we hope somehow to find a trustworthy movie-house owner who will run the film one day, just for us and a few friends. Till then I sleep every night on top of Chaplin."

Now König laughed, too.

"I guess you wouldn't have suspected a decent girl like me of such extravagances?"

Now we both laughed heartily; Rolf, the shepherd, joined in

with a brief howl. König put the Churchill speech on my table, fastened the leash on his dog, said good-bye, and left.

Through the kitchen window I watched them cross the courtyard. A strange couple, I thought, Rolf and Rudolph.

Once more I went with König to his mother's house. König had waited impatiently for a day without ice and snow on the ground. By now it was after New Year's—1945 had begun.

This time he had Rolf with him, and his cart was piled up with books even higher than the last time.

"Won't the cart tip over?" I asked with concern.

"Well, we'll have to be careful. I must take as many books as possible because this might be my last trip."

"What do you mean?"

"The Russians are approaching fast. Who knows how soon they'll be here? My books might go up in flames when the city becomes a battlefield."

"No, no," I said, "it will not come to that."

"Who will stop them?" König asked. "The *Volkssturm,* consisting of fourteen- and sixteen-year-old boys and sixty-year-old men?"

"Of course not. Germany will capitulate before Berlin becomes a battlefield."

"No, it won't," König insisted. "Hitler, the lunatic, will fight, as he has so often assured us, to the last man."

I could not give up. "Hitler will be assassinated by his own people before it comes to the battle of Berlin."

Then, for the first time, I felt König being tough with me when he rather harshly said, "Don't be so naive, Ilse!"

"Why, then, do you take your books to your mother's house

lying east of Berlin?" I asked. "It will be overrun by the Russians earlier than the west where we live."

But König was sure his books would be safer at his mother's house than under the steadily increasing bombardments on the city. "Besides," he argued, "the Russians won't be interested in German literature."

This time the walk took much longer than it had taken on the warm October day three months before. Frequently we had to take out-of-the-way streets, since whole blocks were cordoned off. The skeletons of the bombed-out houses threatened to collapse. There was no longer any part of the city that did not have rows and rows of ruins. Craters in the streets, often filled with water from broken mains, made pulling the cart even more difficult.

And, of course, having Rolf with us didn't make things easier. I held him on a short leash, but often Rolf had his own desires and curiosities. With all his might—and he was a strong dog—he tried to pull me off the sidewalk and into the ruins. But most of the time König, who had developed a special kind of firm tenderness in his voice when talking to the dog, could make Rolf forget whatever had attracted him and walk in step with us.

By now the suburbs had also gotten their share of bombardments. Many houses and many, many beautiful old trees lining the streets were destroyed. I didn't know why, but mutilated trees always had an especially saddening effect on me. Could the reason be that I was cruel enough to have more compassion for a tree than for a human being? A tree seemed so defenseless and innocent to me in comparison with the inhabitants of the villas who, very likely, were members of the Nazi Party. I had the impulse to talk to König about my feelings, but he, shivering with cold, decided to walk more briskly.

Soon we passed the last of the suburban houses and were

walking under a pale, wintry sun that had been hidden by the screen of smoke spread over the city. We walked past open fields where, in October, potatoes had been growing.

Suddenly, König stopped. "Could you wait just for a few minutes, Ilse?" he asked.

And then with a stick and a flat, sharp stone he had picked from the road, he stepped into the field, bent down, and scratched the earth.

"I'm starved," he said, turning to me for a moment with a slightly embarrassed smile. "Forgive me . . . but I must find a potato. There should be some left in the ground."

Fiercely he scratched and dug, taking small steps back and forth. A radiant smile spread over his face when he finally discovered half a potato. Hastily he rubbed off the dirt and bit into it.

"Now I'll find one for you, Ilse," he announced, after he had finished eating.

"No, thank you," I said.

But König fervently continued digging until he found another potato. A large one this time. He took out a handkerchief, cleaned the potato thoroughly, and offered it to me. I think he was glad that I steadfastly refused. It took only a fraction of a minute before he had devoured the whole potato.

Again Mother König greeted us with a warm smile when we arrived, but she seemed startled to see Rolf.

"What's that?" she asked, frowning.

"A dog," König replied. "My dog."

"I can't believe it." And turning to me, Mother König said, "Can you explain?"

But it was König who answered. With pride in his voice, he told his mother how he had gotten the dog and how much he loved him now.

Mother König shook her head. "I don't understand," she murmured. "I don't understand."

The meal was again generous and tasty. Mother König apologized, saying that most of the vegetables were canned now. But it didn't matter. They tasted delicious.

The Kleine König had devoured his first plateful hastily. From the second helping Mother König put on his plate he picked out the carrots, the beans, and the cabbage, but left the potatoes and the sliver of beef untouched.

He met his mother's questioning eyes with a smile. "That's for Rolf," he said.

When we were ready to part, Mother König again gave us several jars to take home. Pointing to an especially large one and giving König an indulgent smile, she said, "This one is for Rolf. It is horse meat."

König was obviously moved, but didn't know what to say. He just embraced his mother tenderly.

We were already outside when she called Rudolph back.

"Please," she urged, "leave the city. It is safer here. Come and stay until the whole mess has blown over. Please."

"Maybe I can come once more with a cart of books," König said.

To more he did not commit himself.

By the time we reached the suburbs it was dark. The sky over the center of the city, however, glowed yellow and orange from fires still burning from the previous night's bombardment. We trudged through deserted streets. The acrid smell of smoldering timbers was so strong I had to tie a handkerchief over my mouth and nose. Once in a while a streetcar, to our amazement still running, passed by, casting a blue light from its blue-painted windows on the pavement. Other streets were turned into streams of filthy water, forcing us to go far out of our way. Rolf trotted silently at our side, getting a comforting word from us every so often.

Exhausted, we reached Meinekestrasse. This time König did not want to come in for a rest. But before saying good-bye, he reached for both my hands. The gesture startled me because intimacies like this were not part of our relationship.

"Ilse," he said pleadingly, "I wish you would leave Berlin. The Russians will be here soon, and you had better get out while it is still possible."

I was astonished. "But König, have you succumbed to the Goebbels propaganda? Do you think the Russians are inhuman beasts? I will welcome whoever comes to liberate us from Hitler and his gang. The sooner the better. I even took some Russian lessons to be able to greet them in a friendly way."

"You'll be better off being liberated by the Americans or the British," he said, still holding on to my hands.

"No," I said sternly. "I'll stay."

Touched by his concern, I freed my hands, lightly stroked his cheek, and said, "Good-bye, Rudolph. Go now."

"All right," he said with a defeated smile. "But please, send a little prayer to God and Prometheus to protect me from fire and ashes on my way home."

These were his last words. His very last words to me.

———

König was not killed by fire or ashes, but by the ever-present wolf inside him: his hunger.

I didn't learn about his end for a long time. Weeks passed during which I didn't hear from him. No visit. No phone call. Nothing. At first I didn't worry. We were all so busy with the everyday struggle, the running after small rations of food, which required standing for hours in long lines at several stores. And often, when your turn came, you were told, *Sorry, we are out of what you want.*

And then there were the air attacks. By now it was the beginning of April, and they came day and night. The Russians were close to the Oder River, approximately forty miles east of Berlin. It was still possible to get out of Berlin toward the south, and most of my friends and acquaintances had left. But a few remained, and we steadily crisscrossed the city to check on each other.

I often thought of the Kleine König. I missed him because I would have liked to talk with him about Kafka's *Castle*, which I had read by now. But since I had no way of contacting him, I comforted myself by assuming that he, too, had left Berlin. Maybe he had tried to reach me when I wasn't home.

Then one day a stranger knocked on my door. She was tall, blond, and blue-eyed, and I was surprised when she introduced herself as König's sister. I asked her in and offered her a cup of tea, apologizing that the tea leaves had been brewed a second time. I waited eagerly to hear why she had come to see me.

Once or twice she took a deep breath and seemed ready to talk. But then she smiled helplessly and said, "I don't know where to begin."

I became very anxious. "How is Rudolph?" I finally asked.

"Oh," she said, "that's it. That's why I am here."

"Is he all right?" I asked.

"I guess he is . . . the poor devil. I guess he's better off than we are . . . being dead."

"Dead?" My voice broke. "Did you say dead?"

"Yes, dead," she said. "He died ten days ago. Mother thought I should come and tell you."

"How did it happen?" I asked, fighting back my tears.

"Well, his end was very different from what I expected it to be."

"You expected it?" I asked.

"Of course, how could he have gotten away with it? With the crazy life he lived, I mean. He was an outlaw, with no respect for law and order; no respect for Hitler and the noble war Hitler is fighting for Germany's future. You must have known something about Rudolph's shameful existence?"

I nodded, but König's sister didn't give me a chance to say anything.

"He would have been caught anyhow," she went on. "Sooner or later. And they would have hanged him." She stopped and shook her head. "How shameful that would have been! For the whole family." She looked at me intently. "Don't you agree?"

I shook my head. "Does your mother agree?"

"Oh, her, she doesn't count," König's sister said, a belittling tone in her voice. "She isn't even a member of the Party."

"But you are?" I asked.

"Certainly, didn't you see?" Her fingers fumbled with the lapel of her jacket. "Oh, my God. I forgot to wear my badge today."

"That's just as well" was all I could think of saying.

"Anyhow," König's sister continued, "as unpleasant as his death was, it was, in my opinion at least, better than being hanged. Or shot."

I was shaken. I wanted to get up and show her out. But I had to know about König's end. "What happened?" I asked.

"Well," she began, "Mother expected Rudolph to bring another load of books. She had saved food all week long to have a big meal for him. I guess you know Rudolph was tortured by his abnormal appetite, hard to satisfy in times like these. Mother saw him, still far away, coming toward the house. He was bent over and walking very slowly, and he stopped frequently. His cart was loaded high, and his dog was tied to it.

"I went out to meet him. He complained about excruciating stomach pains. I helped him into the house, but he fell to the floor before reaching the sofa. Only with difficulty and gasping for air was he able to tell us that, plagued by hunger, he had picked some mushrooms on the roadside and eaten them. I ran outdoors, overturned Rudolph's cart to get rid of the books, and shoved a pillow into it. Then we folded him with bent knees into the cart and, as fast as we could, we pulled the moaning, twisted Rudolph to a small hospital nearby."

Rudolph's sister had spoken rapidly, without emotion. I sat silently, my face buried in my hands.

"Do you want to hear the rest? The end?"

"Yes," I said softly. "I would like to know."

"Arriving at the hospital, we found a large number of wounded soldiers and exhausted refugees lying on the bare ground in front of the entrance. A nurse told us we would have to wait. There were no empty beds, and all the doctors were busy taking care of emergency cases. We waited for a long time, but when it got dark and cold, we decided to take Rudolph home. We folded our jackets over his twitching body. His moaning had gotten weaker and weaker. The dog, though not tied to the cart anymore, had followed us all the way, once in a while licking Rudolph's hand, which hung over the side of the cart. Suddenly the dog let out a long ear-shattering howl and ran off. Rudolph was dead."

König's sister stopped talking. In the long silence that followed, we just exchanged glances.

Then König's sister took a small package out of her handbag. "We found this among Rudolph's books. It says For Ilse . . . in his handwriting."

I opened the package. The first edition of Kafka's "Hunger Artist" lay in my hands.

That very night I read it again. Slowly my eyes took in and savored every word. My ears heard König's voice. And when I neared the end, I even saw him across the room from me in the chair he had been sitting in at his first visit. I saw him clearly with the hunger of his mind and the hunger of his stomach written all over his beautiful, ugly face.

Hope

SHE WAS UGLY. *Extremely ugly. But when you knew Oda, she wasn't ugly anymore. She was very talented: a sculptor and a dancer. She must have been aware of her looks, because she had created masks out of gold or silver foil, which she wore while dancing. The masks were highly stylized and underlined the theme of the dance she was performing: Cassandra, Medusa, the Queen of Sheba.*

Unmasked, Oda's face reflected her personality: she was full of life and joy, and—most charming and characteristic of her—full of hope. A rare combination of attitudes in times of war and suffering.

We all knew she belonged to a small group of people who ran a shortwave radio transmitter. From a rooftop in a Berlin suburb they sent messages to England. Of course, it was a blind operation. They could not know whether and how their messages were received. It was faith and hope that had to carry them through these dangerous activities.

"I hope," Oda told me one day, "that our effort will help to shorten Hitler's Thousand Year Reich." Her dark eyes sparkled. She smiled, nodded, and repeated, "I hope, I hope, I hope!"

Curious about these clandestine activities, I wanted to hear more. But she did not tell me any details.

"Not that I don't trust you, Ilse. It's for your protection only."

Then, for several weeks, nobody in our circle of close friends saw Oda or heard from her.

"Have you seen Oda?" was the first question we asked whenever we saw one another.

"No," was the alarming answer.

One day, however, one of us found out: Oda had been arrested and was in prison. None of us ever heard a word directly from her. We were frightened and we worried.

Only later, much later, a priest who had access to the prison, and who had frequently seen Oda, told me the gruesome facts. In the first few months of her internment, Oda had been composed and dignified. She was full of hope to be eventually released. But as time went on she lost hope and became bitter and uncommunicative. And toward the end—shortly before her hanging—she turned into a fury: full of spite, rage, and hatred.

"And . . ." The priest hesitated a moment before he continued. "And . . . she even became vicious and mean."

I tried to understand, though what I had heard was not at all the picture of Oda I carried in my mind's eye.

"Oda was not a vicious person," I stammered.

The priest, trying to comfort me, said, "Torture and fear can change even the strongest person. We must understand and forgive."

I nodded. But what really went on inside me I could not put into words. My rage and my hatred against the system, the laws, and rules Hitler had imposed on Germany and its people, who so obediently accepted them, grew immeasurably.

Fred

· ⸻ ·

"MARRY ME, marry me, marry me!" pleaded Fred after I had opened the door to let him in.

"But Fred! You love *men*. Remember?"

"Not exclusively. I love you, too."

"Nonsense. You *like* me."

"Marry me," he repeated.

"Why?" I asked, utterly startled by this proposal.

"Because I am drafted. In a few weeks I might be at the front."

"No reason to get married."

He looked at me silently. Then, all of a sudden, his sense of humor and his innate theatricality took over, and he knelt down in front of me.

"Fairest maiden of them all, give me your hand in marriage. Become my war bride."

"And end a friendship of so many years?" I asked, pulling him up to his feet.

"No, no, no!" he said. "Friendship, marriage, love . . . it will all be one. It will be reality and it will be fairy tale. You'll see. It will work. Just say *yes*."

"No," I said, "I won't say yes. You know that very well, Fred. Now stop all this nonsense and tell me—what's going on?"

"It's simple," he said. "I knew it would happen, and now I am drafted."

I had known Fred for several years. He had been the assistant to a filmmaker who catered to every suggestion and wish coming from the Reich's Chancellery—that is, from Goebbels and Hitler. Fred had grudgingly, and often with a bad conscience, stayed with the job because it exempted him from becoming a soldier.

"I will not kill," he had told me. "And I will not fight for Hitler's Thousand Year Reich."

Then came the day he was told he would have to start working on a big documentary called *The Fortress Europe.*

"I don't want to have anything to do with this Nazi propaganda film," Fred had told me, and he had quit his job.

Two weeks later he was drafted.

I took Fred's hand, crossed the corridor, and opened the door to my room. Fred had not visited me for some time, and seeing my room, he broke out laughing.

"What has happened?" he asked. "This isn't a room anymore. It's a park!"

"Well," I said, "I had to do something to fill the empty spaces. I sent most of my furniture to my parents in the provinces where it won't be destroyed in the bombardments."

"Good. You had a few beautiful antique pieces that should survive the Thousand Year Reich."

I nodded. "And now it really is a kind of park."

Fred amused himself by walking around and sniffing the needles of three small blue spruces standing in a row where my Queen Anne secretary had been. He gave the little birch tree a shake; it let some leaves fall to the floor. Large potted ferns lined the wall under the two windows. My canary's cage was hanging in the branches of a small larch tree.

"Where did you get all this greenery?" Fred asked. "And how could you ship your furniture away, when civilians can't get any kind of transportation permit?"

"Connections," I said. "Connections. You know very well, Fred, connections are the miracle workers of these times. A friend of a friend of mine owns a large nursery in Potsdam."

"I see," Fred interrupted, "but a permit to ship your furniture? How did you get that? People can only get them if they are bombed out."

"Exactly." And after a bitter laugh, I added, "Clever, isn't it, to provide a person who is bombed out, and very likely has lost all his furniture, with a transport permit to ship furniture."

"But you were not bombed out, Ilse. So what, for heaven's sake, did you do?"

"Do you remember Franz?"

Fred nodded.

"Well," I explained, "this least of all demanding men, who writes his poetry in a one-room mansard apartment with no furniture except a mattress on the bare floor, one chair, and one table, he was bombed out a few weeks ago."

"I hope he wasn't hurt," Fred said.

"No. Thank goodness. He wasn't home when it happened, and he took his loss quietly and philosophically. 'As long as I have paper, a pencil, and a sound mind, I am all right,' he told me."

I went on to tell Fred how Franz had suggested I should use his transport permit to send my furniture to my parents in Görlitz.

"Great," Fred said. "But isn't it terrible how much of our lives is based on lying and cheating these days? Not only are we lied to and misled every day by our government, we have become liars and cheaters ourselves."

"Even thieves," I added. And in a painful flash, I relived my first theft. I was walking through the KaDeWe, one of Berlin's largest department stores, with a small skein of mending yarn worth only a few pennies clenched in my fist. I needed it urgently to repair my only pair of stockings. I wanted to buy it, but when I handed the yarn and my sheet of coupons to the tall salesgirl, she informed me that my yarn coupons for the month had been used up. I would have to wait three weeks until new coupons were issued. I put the skein on the counter and walked away. A few minutes later, however, I returned. The yarn was still lying on the counter. I waited until the salesgirl was busy with another customer, grabbed the yarn, and walked away. My heart was beating heavily; my cheeks glowed. I lowered my head and stared at the floor. Everybody will see I am a thief, I thought. I walked slowly, just around the counter—I could not yet be accused of stealing. After a few minutes, I headed for the next counter. Still walking slowly, I looked over my shoulder—was someone following me? Several people were behind me. Did they know? Had they seen me taking the yarn? What would my mother think, seeing her daughter, the thief? There was still time to return the yarn, and I would be a decent person again. Then it happened: a hand on my shoulder. My knees wobbled. I stumbled and nearly fell, when the tall salesgirl steadied me. "Miss," she said, "you left your purse on the counter." My tongue was tied. She walked away before I could thank her. Slowly, still trembling, I walked to the exit and entered the street. I was safe now, the skein of yarn still in my sweating fist. But I did not feel good.

And now, half a year later and remembering this hour of the loss of my innocence, I pitied the girl who had become a thief. Should I condemn her? Could I forgive her? I didn't know what to think, but one thought pained me: if I was able to steal, what would become of me later?

Fred's voice drew me from my thoughts. "You know, Ilse, I will have to become an excellent liar, or, to save my self-respect, I could say an excellent performer. Luckily, years ago I took some acting lessons. Those lessons will help me now, and I will succeed."

"Succeed in what?" I asked.

"Succeed in getting myself out of the army. I hate guns and I cannot kill under any circumstances. Besides, I do not think, like Hitler, that we Germans are the super race. His mad dream to subjugate all of Europe must be fought."

"That sounds fine. But how will you get out of the army?"

"I'll think about it day and night, and I'll find a way."

The whole world seemed grim and gray to me when Fred was ready to leave. But since his humor, even in the face of a dark future, never left him completely, he embraced me and said, "And I thought I had a chance to, maybe, make you a young and pretty war widow."

I did not see Fred before he left for the training camp. We only had time for a brief good-bye over the telephone.

"I'll write soon" were his last words.

Weeks passed before I got a letter from him.

Training Camp, Brandenburg
Oct. 12/1944

Dear Ilse,

I am here now for several weeks, and I am fine. However, I feel very sorry for my comrades who have to share the barracks with me. They complain steadily about the stink I cause—and understandably so! You see, Ilse, I wet my bed every night. Though bed is too kind a word for what I'm sleeping on. I'll see the camp doctor tomorrow. I hope it isn't something serious, since I'm eager to be sent to the front. I'll be a brave soldier and fight like a man in battle against the Russians. I do not want them to come to

Berlin and rape you. Goebbels tells us that's what the Russians will be doing.

Sieg Heil, dear Ilse.

Your Fred

I had not digested nor made much sense of this letter when the next one arrived.

Brandenburg, Oct. 16, 1944

My dear Ilse,

Goebbels just informed us over the radio that the "capitalistic gangsters" killed innocent women and children in a monstrous air raid on the western part of Berlin. I worry about you terribly. Please do write soon.

The doctor I saw yesterday diagnosed my bed-wetting as a cold in my bladder. Some medication, he assured me, will take care of it. I certainly hope he's right!

Your Fred

I had no time to write to Fred immediately. My days were filled with running around, trying to get hold of sheets of heavy cardboard. I needed them to replace two large windowpanes shattered a few nights before during a heavy bombardment. I went from store to store. Cardboard Sold Out, read the signs on their doors. I walked through many streets and saw hundreds of glassless windows. I passed gutted houses, the stench of corpses emanating from them.

The sixth store I found was willing to sell me cardboard sheets for an outrageous price. Now I needed nails. To get metal goods I had to apply for a special kind of coupon and then find a store where nails were not sold out. For two nights I leaned the large cardboard sheets against the window frames. The slightest breeze blew them down. Several times during the night, I had to get out of bed and set them up again. Luckily it was a mild October, and during the day I could remove the cardboard and let in the light.

Finally a friend helped me nail the cardboard to the window frames. The result, of course, was darkness. How to cope with it? I cut a square of about twenty-by-twenty inches into each piece of cardboard and taped "hinges" on one side of the squares. Now, during the day, I could fold the squares back like little doors.

This done, I was ready to write a note to Fred when another letter from him arrived.

Brandenburg, Oct. 24th, 44

Ilse, my dear,

I have bad news. My bed-wetting has not been cured yet, and now something is wrong with my bowels, too. I cannot hold them. It happens frequently, mostly in bed at night, that I have to let them go. The whole barracks complains bitterly about the smell! As a result, I was transferred to a single room, a cell really, a kind of small cabin behind the main barracks. It saddens me to be separated from my dear comrades. All of them fine fellows, ready and enthusiastic to fight for their Führer and their beloved Fatherland. I can only hope that the specialist I'll be seeing tomorrow will diagnose my malady and find the right cure.

I'm waiting eagerly for a word (or two!) from you, my dear Ilse.

Greetings and Heil Hitler!
Your Fred

Berlin W. 15, Oct. 28/44

My dear, poor Fred,

I got your three letters, and I feel ever so sorry for you.
Besides, I am startled! I cannot understand. As long as I
have known you, you've been always so healthy. Remember
how I used to kid you about your horse stomach? How I
envied you because of it! Nothing, not even the lousy bread,
which, as we know, has sawdust added to it, and against
which my stomach rebels terribly, not even that could upset
yours.

What is it, Fred, that makes you suddenly so susceptible
and so ill?

If there is something—anything—I can do for you,
please let me know.

Get well soon,

Your Ilse

I was ready to put my letter in an envelope and mail it when
I suddenly had a second thought. I, of course, knew Fred's letters
speaking of his eagerness to get to the front and fight for Führer
and Fatherland were a sham. He assumed letters leaving the camp
would go through controls and be read. But what about his "mal-
adies"? Were they real?

I destroyed my letter and, assuming also letters coming to the
camp might be read, I started a new one.

Berlin W. 15, Oct. 28/44

My dear, poor Fred,

I got your three letters and my heart goes out to you
on hearing about your condition. I know your health was
always delicate, and when you were drafted I worried about

it and asked myself: will he be physically strong enough to become the brave soldier he so much wants to be? Now I see your health is playing tricks on you. But, though it saddens me, I also know that your determination and positive attitude will help you overcome these temporary afflictions. Your wish to be at the front soon will come true.

We here, after the heavy bombardment of the western part of the city, are in good spirits again, knowing that these air gangsters will, as Speer and Goebbels promise us, soon be stopped by our *Wunderwaffe*. Berlin will be rebuilt to be more beautiful than it ever was before. I personally suffered a small loss: the glass in my two windows was shattered. But I've already replaced it with strong cardboard sheets. I don't complain, because it is a small sacrifice compared to the greater sacrifices you and others bring for Germany's victory.

We two understand each other, don't we?

Your Ilse

Fred's next letter arrived soon.

Brandenburg, November 1st, 1944

Dear Ilse,

Your dear letter did me good. If the "Homefront" is as cheerful and brave as you are, I, and all of us soldiers, know what we are fighting for.

Heil Hitler!

Your Fred

This short letter disappointed me. It was no clue to anything, and Fred's next letter was a real puzzle.

Brandenburg, Nov. 4th/44

Dear Ilse,

My physical condition has improved a bit, though I'm still kept in isolation. However, something else is happening to me that frightens me even more. Maybe it is only the aftermath of my wretchedness, but it's terrifying anyhow. Nightmares! Horrible, horrible nightmares from which I awaken bathed in sweat. I hope to overcome them, so, for now, I will not burden you with their contents.

Please write and tell me what is going on in your mind behind the papered-up windows in your parklike room. How I wish I could be there!

Your Fred

Berlin, Nov. 7th

Dear Fred,

My papered-up window (notice: I say *window* only), on which I painted a large sun, does not let light shine through. But . . . the other window does! I was beginning to worry whether my "little park" was getting enough light to stay green when my father brought me a huge pane of glass. An arduous task with the trains overcrowded with soldiers. He had to fabricate quite a story to get a travel permit.

Now I have, for a few hours at least, enough daylight to paint a little. It saves my soul and also brings me some money. I was extremely lucky to find an art dealer who buys my paintings though I am not a member of the Nazi Art Association. Bless him!

However, why people buy paintings to hang on walls, which might collapse any minute, is a real puzzle to me.

I would so like to see you, Fred! Is it possible for me to come and visit?

Your Ilse

P.S. I wanted not to inquire about your nightmares, since you didn't want to talk about them; but I have to. Fred, please tell me what they are about. Friends must share things. Joys and sufferings.

Your Ilse

Dearest Ilse-friend,

I might just as well tell you about my nightmares. Especially since they have become so intolerable that I've had to turn to my comrades and ask them to help me. This is what happens: Every night I have this horrible dream that Hitler is a madman. Imagine, Hitler, our adored Führer, to whom we owe so much! I dream he will bring ruin to Germany. I tell my comrades, and they look at me in disgust. I tell them also, I know I am a madman to have such dreams, and plead for understanding and help. But nobody comes toward me when I stretch out my trembling hands. Instead, they turn their backs and walk away. Only one fellow, a small and timid one, came to me and advised me to talk to the commander of our camp.

I thanked him for his good idea, and an hour later I talked to the commander. "Help me!" I implored him. "Do something to rid me of these frightening dreams. They stand so much in contrast to my daytime thoughts and beliefs!" He could not help me, but he did refer me to the staff psychiatrist.

That's how it stands right now, Ilse. I'll write after my session with the psychiatrist.

With love,

Your Fred

Berlin, Nov. 14th/44

Dear Fred,

I must talk to you. Please, tell me whether, and if so when, I can come to visit. I've asked you before—this time, please answer.

Ilse

I waited eagerly for an answer, but before I could have received one, another letter from Fred arrived. I could hardly decipher his hasty handwriting.

Brandenburg, Nov. 14th.

Dear Ilse,

I have only a few minutes to write this note before I have to hand it to a fellow who is visiting his brother here—he will smuggle this letter out of the camp. I beg you to act quickly! I need vomiting powder—a pharmacist will advise you what to buy. I have faith in your ingenuity to think of a proper disguise for mailing it to me. Act quickly, please!

Fred ended his letter with the cryptic remark:

Success and victory will be mine soon. Be proud of your loving friend Fred.

I immediately went to a pharmacy and asked whether I could get vomiting powder. I was a bit nervous. Would the clerk ask me why I wanted it?

But he only said, "Oh, yes. *Pulvera di vomicose,* that's what you want. How much of it?"

"Oh, just a couple of grams," I said, and a few minutes later I left the store.

Now I had to figure out in what kind of a disguise to send it to Fred. I could leave it in the small vial I had bought it in and replace the label with one saying Talcum Powder. No good, I said to myself, the amount is too small. Put it in a white unmarked envelope maybe? No, suspicious, too. Finally I had an idea for which I would need a larger amount of vomiting powder than I had bought.

I went to another pharmacy and bought several more grams of the powder. Thank goodness no coupons were needed for this purchase. I hurried home. In my kitchen I found a small, empty glass jar, which I took into the bathroom. Luckily I had bought a tube of toothpaste, coupon required, a few days before. I did not touch the lid, but carefully opened the bottom of the tube with the help of a small pair of pliers. Then, with my toothbrush, I removed the toothpaste very carefully from the tube, placing it in the glass jar. After I had emptied the tube as well as I could, I washed it out and let it dry thoroughly. Afterward, I filled it with the vomiting powder. While rolling up the bottom of the tube again, I suddenly became aware that I was humming one of Fred's favorite songs: "Lili Marlene." I had to laugh at myself.

The short note I added to the small package to Fred I signed Ilse Marlene.

I was disappointed not to hear from Fred for a whole week. But then, without any further words from him, I received a permit to visit him the following Sunday at three in the afternoon. With an anxious heart, I looked forward to this meeting. After an hour's train ride through the pine woods surrounding Berlin, I arrived at Brandenburg.

I had no trouble finding the training camp. At its entrance, I was thoroughly inspected and had to fill out a form explaining the reason for my visit. To see an old friend, I wrote.

"This is the barrack for dangerous comrades," said the young soldier who led me to a small building far behind the main barracks.

Fred . . . dangerous? I mused.

"How dangerous is he?"

"Well, it's not enough that he stinks up the barracks, he also has these strange ideas about our Führer."

"Ideas?" I asked. "He wrote me he just has dreams, nightmares that frighten him."

"Dreams or ideas, what's the difference? I think our commander did right to put him in isolation. Who knows? He could infect the others."

I was horrified to see that the door to Fred's small cabin had been padlocked. The young soldier unlocked it. "Go in now," he said. It sounded like an order. "In thirty minutes I'll be back to fetch you. Heil Hitler."

The door flew open immediately. Fred's arms caught me in a wild embrace. I didn't even have a chance to look at his face. He held me tight for quite some time.

Over his shoulder I could see the small room: a wooden chair in front of a small wooden table, two narrow windows without curtains, a bunk bed, and a wash basin with a shelf above it—no adornments at all.

"Fred," I said, "let me see you."

With great effort, I freed myself from his embrace, stepped back, and looked at him. The gray, badly fitted uniform hung loosely over Fred's thin body. His gaunt face was dominated by his almost black, piercing eyes. Small eyes, sitting close together, gave him a kind of monkeylike look. No harm in that. Monkeys were among my favorite creatures.

For the first time, I found Fred at a loss for words.

Finally Fred broke the silence. "Ilse?" he asked, his voice low. "Ilse?" he asked again.

I could see he was moved. I was touched. This was a Fred I did not know at all. I wanted to smile, but I couldn't. It took some time before a smile flicked across Fred's face.

He took a deep breath, which seemed to transform him into the Fred I knew, and laughing, he asked, "How do I look to you, Ilse? Pitiful, I hope."

I had not quite adjusted myself to the strangeness of the situation. I just nodded, still unable to smile.

But Fred's voice, hushed, was joyous now. "Ilse, I have made it! I have played my role well. I am considered, and obviously diagnosed as, a madman. A dangerously unbalanced one at least. They'll not send me to the front."

And then, with his usual ebullience, Fred grabbed me and whirled me around, knocking over the chair and upsetting his high boots standing beside the bed.

"Fred," I pleaded. "We only have a half hour—let's talk."

"Is that all the time those bastards will give you?"

"Yes, so please, be serious now. Tell me why you wanted the vomiting powder so urgently."

"Ilse, you are wonderful! To send a tube of toothpaste! It didn't arouse the slightest suspicion."

"But why?" I asked again. "Why vomiting powder?"

"Maybe I didn't tell you that a general was due to come to inspect our camp. And, of course, to inspect us. I thought it would be a splendid idea to vomit on the general's uniform when he was mustering us and passing me."

"And did you?"

"Of course I did. And to great effect. Immediately I was removed from the line and brought to the infirmary. And there, just when the doctor approached me, I was able to vomit once more, on his shoes. Isn't that wonderful?"

I nodded. "But what will happen to you now?"

"I'll have to play it very smart," Fred explained. "I will, step by step, give up bed-wetting and thank the physician profusely for having cured my bowels. But I will, frequently and to everybody, express my real thoughts dressed up as nightmares, as dreams that torture me and let me doubt my own sanity."

Fred looked at me triumphantly. "Do you approve, Ilse?"

"Of course I do. But won't it be hard to play this role for any length of time?"

"Not for me, Ilse. Don't worry, I'll manage. Besides, I have a goal: I want to be eventually transferred to a sanatorium in the Black Forest. A place where borderline cases not yet ready for sterilization or extinction are kept and treated."

"Does such a place exist?" I asked. "How do you know about it?"

"There is one fellow here who is one of us. He is trustworthy. His father is an anti-Nazi and holds a high position in the army. He knows about this sanatorium, and he is trying to maneuver his son into it."

There was a knock at the door, a key rattled, the door was flung open, and a tall soldier filled the narrow doorframe.

"A girl?" he said in disbelief. "A girl?"

"Show him your pass," said Fred.

The intruder studied it carefully. "All right. Twenty more minutes are left."

He banged the door shut and locked it. We heard him walk away.

"What was that all about?" I asked.

"Nothing. They just check up on me every once in a while. Isn't it idiotic?" Fred laughed out loud.

I, however, couldn't laugh: a knot seemed to close my throat.

"Tell me about yourself," Fred urged. "Tell me what you paint."

"Oh, you know, nothing that's close to my heart, just kitsch paintings for quick sales. I need the money. I haven't told you yet that I quit my half-day job as a secretary when my boss was transferred to Paris. I did not want to go with him. I would not like to be part of the German occupation power."

"Of course," Fred agreed. And with a bitter laugh he added, "Imagine! The swastika over the Louvre."

Fred, in anticipation of my visit, had managed to save some bitter malt coffee, cold by now. But with aplomb, he served it. He set a tin mug and a water glass on white doilies he had cut out of toilet paper. I unwrapped a few oat cookies I had baked the night before.

"They aren't sweet enough," I apologized. "Recently the sugar ration was cut drastically and—"

"It's sweet enough to have a coffee-klatsch with you, Ilse." Fred put his arm around my shoulder and kissed my cheek tenderly. "Would you still say no if I would ask you again to marry me?" Fred said, staring at the ceiling.

"I think I would," I replied, raising my eyes to the ceiling, too.

What I saw there made me smile. Pasted on the low ceiling, directly over Fred's cot, was a photo of me. It was an enlargement of my face taken out of a group photograph Fred had taken some time ago.

"I need someone to talk to," he explained with an impish smile.

I didn't know what to say. I was moved and upset. I had very tender feelings for Fred, but I wanted him to consider me nothing more than a friend.

We sat in silence, staring at the ceiling.

"Now I have to worry about you, Ilse." Fred sounded serious.

"No, you don't," I said.

"But you quit your job, and since the government is talking about mobilizing women for the war effort, you might be called."

"I've thought of that, and I have taken steps."

"Don't be mysterious, Ilse, what steps?"

"Well, I've composed and typed a letter in which my boss—"

"You mean your ex-boss," Fred interjected.

"—in which my ex-boss set up a schedule obligating me to send him weekly reports to Paris."

"Did your ex-boss sign this letter?"

I shrugged my shoulders, smiling.

Fred put his hand under my chin and turned my face to his.

"I hope you didn't—"

"No, I didn't fake his signature, I had it already. Some time ago he signed a blank sheet of stationery on which I was supposed to send a message to a client of his. Since I delivered this message by phone, I did not need the signed, empty stationery."

Fred applauded. "Smart little Ilse."

"Of course, my ex-boss doesn't know that I am still employed by him; but the letter will be evidence should I ever be drafted for any kind of work."

"But you don't have any salary," said Fred with great concern.

"Don't worry, my paintings take care of that. They sell like hotcakes."

"Amazing," said Fred.

"No, it isn't. People have money, paper money which the government prints at random and in quantity. Of course it's worthless outside of Germany, but here it has buying power. And since there aren't many things to purchase anymore and paintings can be bought without coupons, people buy them. You see, Fred, I've become a war profiteer."

Fred laughed. "What do you do with all that money?"

"Well, since I don't belong to the Nazi Art Association, I can buy paints and brushes only on the black market for enormous prices. Besides, we have to buy food for several people, living underground."

"Who is 'we'?"

"Oh, I guess I haven't told you about Oskar yet. Well, Oskar and I have become thick friends. I had to swear to him not to tell anybody about him and especially his activities—and I haven't, not even you. But now I think I can tell you. Oskar prints food ration cards, and sometimes I help him. In the basement of the house he lives in we—"

At that moment the door was unlocked. The soldier who had brought me to Fred's cabin had come to collect me.

"Time is up," he said. "But I'll give you another minute to say good-bye." And in what he must have considered an act of discretion, he turned his back to us.

That, of course, didn't give me a chance to finish my sentence. It turned Fred into a living question mark. After a hasty and cliché-laden good-bye, Fred said, "Heil Hitler," and, whispering in my ear, advised me to say Heil Hitler, too.

But I didn't. Long ago I had made an oath to myself never to allow these words to come from my lips. Instead, I gave Fred an extra loud kiss in order to satisfy the generous soldier who stood facing the door and said, "Forget me not."

My guide walked slowly, trying to involve me in a conversation. But I was too stirred up and too worried about Fred's future to talk.

Two or three more short letters from Fred arrived. They had nothing to say but how glad he was to have seen me.

I wrote a couple of letters, too, inquiring how he was, but for several weeks I did not hear from him at all. Then, at last, a thick letter arrived. The postal stamp did not reveal where it had come from, but it was drastically different from the postal stamp of the training camp in Brandenburg. I guessed the letter had come from the so-called sanatorium in the Black Forest. It had.

Sanatorium, Dec. 20, 1944

Dear Ilse,

How are you? I am fine, but how I wish you could be here, too. Most of the inmates are people like you and me—enthusiastic Nazis. The labor we have to do is not backbreaking, but tedious. All kinds of manual work. Folding pamphlets and inserting them into envelopes. The pamphlets assure the German population of the soon-to-come victory of our army. It certainly cheers you up to know you are helping to spread this good news to your countrymen. Occupational skills of the inmates are used to good advantage. Tailors, for instance, repair uniforms shipped to us from the front. But for some bloodstains and bullet holes, they are still in perfect condition. Many of them really brand-new. Isn't it wonderful to know a dead soldier can still be of use, and help, to a living one by passing on his uniform?

The only life-threatening thing here is wasps. Since we are housed in what was once a farmer's stable, there are—surprisingly enough—still lots of them around. They swarm around your head and your food while you are eating. We are steadily reminded to watch each single spoonful of our meatless potato soup from the moment it is scooped out of the tin bowl till it is at our lips. But in spite of these warnings, a comrade, a fast and greedy eater, died a few days ago. He obviously had swallowed a wasp and, before the doctor arrived, died from suffocation. It was a grim scene to watch, which I'll never forget. One of the inmates though was kind enough to console me. The mind of this dead chap, he told me, was so far gone that he very likely would soon have been evaluated as incurable and a burden to society. He would, if he was lucky, not have been put away but only sterilized.

I guess you agree, Ilse: This is a fine solution to protect and improve the German race.

No threat like that hangs over me. Be sure, dear Ilse Marlene, I will survive our soon-to-come glorious victory and live happily in the remaining 990 years of the Thousand Year Reich.

Heil Hitler!

Your Fred

Berlin, Dec. 29/1944

Dear Fred,

Finally, after a long wait, your letter arrived. I'm glad you seem content. But I would like to hear much more.

What are your nights like? Can you sleep through them, or do you have air raids, too?

Christmas came and went. Not many people were in the mood to celebrate. I had Christa and the Kleine König over for the evening. I even lit three candles on one of my little pines. "Dangerous," the Kleine König warned. "The needles are so dry already." So I extinguished them, and we sang a couple of carols.

We Berliners are living through harrowing days and nights on our way to victory. Almost daily we are "visited." In the daytime the Americans drop their bombs on us. And at night the British do their murderous job.

I had a bad scare. A few nights ago a heavy air raid was announced over the radio. I, of course, did not go to the basement shelter, but I did not undress before going to bed. Then, quite suddenly, it happened. A blast! An ear-shattering roar! Another blast! Then blast after blast. Second after second. I know you never hear the bomb that kills you. Small comfort, however, when the walls start shaking and the mortar trickles from the ceiling.

I pulled my bedding over my head, which hardly dulled the thundering blasts. It went on and on. An eternity it seemed. When it finally stopped, I pulled the cover off my head, but had to slip back under it immediately because the air in the room was so dense with mortar dust that I could hardly see the opposite wall. Trembling, I stayed under the covers, waiting. I was surprised to still be alive. Not even hurt! But somehow I had no desire to crawl out from under the feathery cave surrounding my head and face life. When, after a long time, I finally did, I saw the door and its frame torn out of the wall, the ceiling lamp dangling on its cord, my bookshelves off the wall, and books strewn all over the floor. Everything was white with a heavy layer of dust.

Fred, can you believe that at that moment I felt nothing? Nothing but a great listlessness. I didn't even want to get up. Instead I sought refuge in sleep and did something I seldom do: I swallowed a sleeping pill. Maybe, I thought, when I wake up tomorrow, it will turn out to have been a dream.

Of course, when morning came, I had to face reality. The first thing I saw was my canary. The delicate cage was miraculously intact, but the bird lay dead on its back. The air pressure of the bomb blast must have burst its little lungs.

I had just fetched a bucket of water and rags to start cleaning up when I heard a knock from the corridor. It was Rudolph. With a sigh of relief he grasped both my hands. "Why didn't you answer the phone?" he wanted to know. "What a silly question," he said immediately, seeing the devastation around me. He was still breathless from running the greater part of the way to my place.

No transportation in the western part of the city was functioning. He told me how worried he was when the morning news described what they called "the infamous attack" on the western section inhabited by civilians only. Of course, they did not mention the railroad station Zoo which, as you know, is just a stone's throw from where I live and is a target worth hitting.

Well, the Kleine König and I didn't talk much. We threw ourselves into the cleanup.

Not more than fifteen minutes had passed when there

was another knock. It was Christa. She flung her arms around my neck. "Thank God" was all she said. Then, surveying the situation with one glance, she took off her coat, rolled up her sleeves, and reached for the water-filled bucket. I was startled. Christa, this delicate, elegant little person—you know how she still manages to dress with such style—Christa got down on her knees and began scrubbing the floor. And, imagine, she even started to sing a long-forgotten children's song about the washerwomen who wash and wash and wash all day and remain happy and gay.

The greatest problem, of course, was the door. König and I had pressed the door frame back into the wall, but it wasn't well secured.

"If we hold our breath," König said, "it will stay awhile."

We had not made much progress when I heard another knock from the corridor and there was your friend Sven. You once told me he is a silent admirer of mine. I didn't recognize him right away because the white batiste handkerchief that always adorns his breast pocket was tied over his mouth and nose to protect him from the flying cinders in the street. He was overflowing with sympathy and pity on seeing the mess in my place.

You know our dear Sven can be a bit long-winded at times, and I was a bit nervous, maybe even unfriendly. I was so eager to go back to work, and I knew very well that Sven, in his navy blue pinstriped suit, was neither ready nor willing to join the cleanup crew. However, he had his own way of endearing himself. With a measured gesture, he unbuttoned the shiny brass buttons of his overcoat and said, "Now you see it—now you don't." He let us have just a glimpse of the top of a bottle squeezed into the inside pocket of his coat. Immediately he closed the coat again, turned to each of us with a nod and a smile asking whether we could "lay off" for a while to celebrate life. We shouted yes in unison. Sven took out the bottle again and uncorked it. He held it out at arm's length for us to read the label: Vodka. Genuine Russian vodka.

"Soon we will have a lot of it," he said.

"That's a promise I like," said Christa. She reached for the bottle and raised it to her lips.

"No, no, no! Not like that," I said, knowing Sven would not approve of such vulgarity. "I'll fetch some glasses."

I had to wipe them carefully. The mortar dust had even penetrated the kitchen cabinet doors.

Sven generously filled the glasses—they were wine-glasses!—and after we had emptied them greedily, body and mind were warmed up quickly. Christa, who had started to flirt with Sven, asked him for another sip, and when he poured her just a sip, she shook her pretty head, leaned it on Sven's shoulder and held up her skimpily filled glass. Sven filled it nearly to the brim.

The Kleine König and I got another drink, too, and soon we were all laughing and singing as if the world were just a bowl of roses. Of course, not much more work was done. By now the bottle was nearly empty and then the exhilaration of having survived, of still being alive—and silliness!—took over. Christa danced a wild Charleston and asked me to join her. I tried, but I'm not good at doing the Charleston. Sven pretended to play the clarinet, and König and I clapped our hands and marveled at Christa's elegance and endurance. She went on and on until finally, rather breathless, she threw herself at Sven's chest and asked for another vodka.

Sven obliged but asked for another Charleston in exchange. Christa declared he could have a rumba only. She tried to make him fall in step with her, but Sven declined, and remembering he had an appointment, he said good-bye and rather abruptly left, keeping his posture and his dignity.

By now we were so tipsy we needed a bite to eat. Luckily I had bought my weekly cheese ration a day before and could make three little sandwiches. We had hardly swallowed the last bite when the air-raid sirens sounded. Christa and the Kleine König rushed to the Zoo bunker, and I, exhausted, flopped down on my couch and pulled a pillow over my spinning head.

That's all for today. But there's something I didn't tell you, Fred. Something was missing at our life-celebrating festivities. It was you. I really missed you very much! Write soon.

Your Ilse

I never received an answer to this last letter of mine. I could not even be sure whether my letter had reached Fred. The war, with its steadily increasing bombardments, put more and more strain on everybody. Chaos and havoc reigned and, of course, mail service, though still functioning, was unreliable.

However, I did not worry too much. And as it later turned out after the war's end, I was right in believing Fred to be safe where he was. Safer, at least, than we were in Berlin, which became the last battlefield of the war.

About six weeks after Germany's capitulation, Fred stood one day in front of my door. He was, as usual, full of stories about extraordinary events he had witnessed on his two-hundred-mile foot march through a great part of Germany. Devastation and ruins were everywhere. But his remarkable ability to look for— and find!—comfort and hope for the future had kept him in good spirits. He had hardly changed, and I was glad to see him.

"I guess you still refuse to marry me?" he asked.

"I guess you are right," I said.

Fear

*F*EAR. *How to overcome it? I had tried; but I had failed.*
At best I could suppress or hide it. But it was ever present. Just
like the wolf of hunger, it was a beastly something inside me, always
ready to take over. Body and soul.

Nearly every night the fierce, ear-piercing howl of the air-raid
sirens cut into me. It frightened me just as much as it frightened
everybody else. But the face I showed to the people around me—
even to my friends—was a smiling face. At least most of the time.
Though I was calm on the outside, fear nestled deeply inside me.

I also trembled with fear each time I turned the corner from the
Kurfürstendamm into my street: Would my house still be there or
had the bombardment during the few hours I had been away reduced
it to rubble? Was it a friend who knocked at my door or the Gestapo
to arrest me? Just the other day I had talked freely to a storekeeper
about my feelings for Hitler. He could have denounced me. I had
trusted the storekeeper because he, grim-faced, had told me his
seventeen-year-old son had been drafted. But was a grim face enough
to take him for an anti-Nazi? I should not be so trusting, I knew.
I also knew that there were many provocateurs around.

Keep your mouth shut, Ilse!
Fear, fear, fear.

There were also moments of frightening illusions. One night I
was torn out of deep sleep by the air-raid sirens, and passing a

mirror, something extraordinary happened: the mirror did not reflect me. For a fleeting second, I saw an Ilse-child. And when I stepped closer to investigate, the image suddenly changed to an ancient, ashen Ilse-face. Where was I? The mirror refused to show me the thirty-year-old Ilse. Did I dream? I put my face so close to the mirror that my nose touched the cold glass. And then, inch by inch, I stepped back until a startled and frightened face—myself—appeared.

Since I wanted to escape fear, I sometimes sought refuge in drink. And sometimes it helped . . . for a few hours. But even this relief was accompanied by fear: Was the liquor I had bought on the black market safe? It could contain wood alcohol. I had heard of blindness, paralysis, and even death as a result of drinking wood alcohol.

Fear, fear, fear.

Nothing, however, nothing cut deeper into my heart than the fear for my friends. Were they still alive? The hours after every bombardment while waiting to hear from them, the often unsuccessful attempts to reach them by phone, were worse than the bombardment itself. For my parents and my grandmother, living far to the east of Berlin, I felt I needn't fear. No bombs had fallen there and, up to the last days of April 1945, when the Russian army rolled over that part of Germany, they were relatively safe.

And then there were those not strong enough to keep their fears to themselves. I was pulled into the suffering of a stranger one night. A frail middle-aged woman and I were the only passengers on a dimly lit streetcar rattling along the Kurfürstendamm. The windows of the streetcar were painted blue so that no light would be visible from the outside. A few minutes after I had entered and settled down, the woman, who had been sitting far in the back, rose from her seat and came to sit down beside me.

In a hushed voice, after looking round to check whether anybody was in earshot—though there was not another single soul in the car—she whispered, "Do you know whether they are coming?"

I knew what she meant: Had I heard a forewarning on the radio? Were enemy planes on their way to Berlin?

"No," I said, "I haven't heard."

A long silence—during which, inch by inch, she moved closer to me—ended by her asking, "Aren't you afraid?"

"No," I said. Trying to console her, I put my hand on her knee. Eagerly she reached for my hand and pressed it hard.

"I live close to the Zoo railroad station," she explained.

"So do I," I told her.

"You know what that means, don't you?" she asked, her voice shaking.

Of course I knew that this station was a target for the Allied bombers. But I shrugged and very casually told her that the Allies were not very good at precision bombing. Seeing the fearful face of this woman, I would have been willing to tell a lot more lies.

And then she could not hold back anymore, and a stream of tears wetted my hand, which she pressed to her chest.

Vera

I RECOGNIZED her handwriting immediately. It was beautiful. It was large and straight with just a light slant toward the left. Clear and without any flourish, just like Vera herself, I thought, holding the unopened envelope in my hand. My heart began to pound. We had been friends many years ago—twelve years ago, I realized with a certain shock—when we were classmates in the Latin school in Görlitz.

I had adored her, and so had the whole class. We all agreed: she was not only the smartest, but also the prettiest girl among us. Reddish blond curly hair framed her pale, lightly freckled face. Her hair was cut short, much shorter than the fashion of the time dictated, and that added something special to her looks. It made me think of a Greek boy whose bust I had seen in my history book. Since her father was a well-to-do lawyer, she was always beautifully and expensively dressed. There was another rich girl in our class, always boasting and showing off her outfits and making the rest of us feel like Cinderellas. But Vera was kind and considerate. Though self-assured, she never drew attention to herself. She sometimes even apologized when one of us admired a new dress she wore.

"Oh," she once said, "I don't know. I really didn't want this dress. But Mother bought it anyhow and insisted I wear it to school."

Then she turned to Lisa, the daughter of a poor shopkeeper

in the suburbs, and complimented her on her new hair ribbon. "This pale blue goes so well with the color of your pretty eyes," she said. It caused Lisa to blush with pride.

All that happened long ago. After I left Görlitz for Berlin, Vera and I drifted apart. Every once in a while, at Christmas or Easter, we exchanged greetings.

But now it was neither Christmas nor Easter. It was April 1944 when I held Vera's letter in my hand. I opened it.

Dear Ilse,

Next week I will be in Berlin. Would you allow me to visit you? If you want to see me, please let me know. But don't write to me. My parents are gone, and I do not live on Bruckstrasse anymore. Please, just write a card, a short greeting, nothing else, to Alma Reuter, Feldweg 7, Jauernick, Silesia. Do not mention my name at all.

With love and many fond memories,
Your Vera

I had to read this letter again. Allow her to visit me? How strange. I was mystified. It did not sound like Vera, who always used to express herself so clearly. It was only on a second reading that I discovered a P.S. on the back of the sheet.

Should it be too risky for you to receive me, do not respond at all. I will fully understand and will keep you in my heart, hoping to see you later when better times arrive.

In the meantime, forget me not.
Your Vera

And then, slowly, a veil began to lift. I remembered our school days: Once a week, when an hour of religious instruction was on the schedule, our class was broken up. Most of us were Protestants. Catholics and Jews got their lesson in separate classrooms. Vera joined the group of four Catholics. Only two girls were Jewish. I also remembered that many West European Jews had, long ago, converted to Catholicism. So Vera could be Jewish. *My parents are gone,* she wrote. To a concentration camp? I wondered. And she, nameless, was staying with a friend. Hiding?

I immediately sent a card to Alma Reuter. And, knowing that mail sometimes got lost, I wrote a second one the following day.

Then I waited.

It took two weeks before Vera arrived. Timid and not self-assured as I knew her, she stood in front of my door. The twelve years during which I had not seen her had not diminished her beauty. However, the radiance in her face was gone, replaced by a haunted look. Her hair was longer now and not as well groomed as it used to be. The overstuffed rucksack on her back contrasted with her elegant but worn dress.

We fell into each other's arms.

"Are you sure you want me here?" Vera asked.

I nodded. "Of course," I said.

"I won't stay long." And rather casually she added, "I'm on my way to Spain."

"To *Spain?*" I asked, startled.

"Yes, to Spain. I hope I'll make it."

"I'm happy to have you here, Vera. You can stay as long as you want to. But first take off your rucksack and—"

Vera did not let me finish. "First you must tell me something, Ilse. Do you know I am Jewish?"

"To be honest . . . I wasn't quite sure. But it does not make a difference to me."

"Oh, yes, it does. It is against the law to give shelter to Jews. You must know that."

"Of course I know. But their laws don't apply to me. Come on, Vera, take off your rucksack and relax."

"Can I stay overnight?" Vera asked shyly.

"Of course you can! This couch is very wide. We both will sleep comfortably."

I helped Vera take off her rucksack. Its weight was tremendous. After I put her down in my easy chair, Vera kicked off her shoes. Her feet were swollen, and there was a bloodstain on her stocking.

"How did you get here?" I asked. "Did you walk?"

"Most of the way. The controls in the trains are very thorough now. But . . . I still can get by. I'm not wearing the mandatory yellow Star of David, and my identity card does not yet carry the mandatory added name Sarah."

I turned my face away. I did not want Vera to see how upset I was and how sorry I felt for her.

"Are you sure you want me to stay?" she asked again.

"I am very sure. But before you tell me more, you must let me fix a bite for you—for us, I mean. You also can take a bath. Today is Saturday, one of the days when we have hot water."

"A bath," she said, glee in her voice.

I left Vera alone, went to the kitchen, and carefully put together a meager meal out of food scraps I had in my pantry. When I came back, Vera was stretched out on my couch after her bath.

"It's paradise," she said. And for a second, a relaxed and delighted smile took twelve years off her face.

"Come, Vera, you must be hungry. Let's eat."

"I shouldn't eat. I have no food ration coupons to give you."

"I don't want any," I said. "But tell me, how did you manage to eat on your way to Berlin?"

"My rucksack is full of things I can give to people in exchange for a slice of bread. Or, when I'm lucky, for a meal." She took a few bites. "I'm sure, Ilse, I'll have some things to give to you."

I shook my head firmly. "No, no. I don't want anything. I'm glad you are here."

We didn't talk while eating, and after we had finished, we still didn't talk. I was burning to hear what had happened to her and her parents, but Vera kept silent. Her large blue eyes looked around my room, taking in everything. When she saw a picture of Dodo, my grandmother, hanging on the wall, she got up and caressed Dodo's face. Wordless. Our eyes met and we smiled at each other. The silence seemed to grow and grow. I waited for her to break it. I didn't want to ask questions that would pierce her heart.

Finally, in a low voice, Vera said, "Maybe it's better I don't tell you all. Better for you, I mean. It will only upset you."

"But I would like to know, if it isn't too painful for you to tell."

"I'll tell you the facts, as briefly as I know how."

Then Vera told how her father had gradually lost most of his clients. A few friends still came for advice, but they came at night. Regulations against Jews got stricter and stricter. Then her father was approached by the Party. They wanted him to join the Judenrat, which meant he would not be transported as long as he helped to catch Jews and bring them "to justice"—as the Party put it. He refused, even though he knew this would mean he and his family would be on a transport within a very short time. And he prepared for it: he got bullets for his revolver. "I will not let them take me and your mother alive," he told Vera. "But you must live. Here is the address of a friend in Madrid. Somehow you must make your way to him. You look like an Aryan, and you are an intelligent girl. You will succeed. You must try to get yourself a B.D.M. uniform, and everybody will take you for a *Deutscher Mädchen.* Mother has packed her jewelry along with other valuables in this rucksack. It's worth a fortune, and it will save your life."

Vera stopped.

I pulled her close to me. I held her hands and waited.

In great trepidation she continued.

"I don't want you to hear the two shots," her father said the following day. "You must leave tomorrow before daybreak. But before you start your long and hazardous trek to Spain, go to Alma Reuter. She's a good soul, and she was a faithful servant to us. Use her name and address to make some contacts." Berlin, he told Vera, would be a good place to sell some of the jewelry.

At that moment my doorbell rang.

"Do you expect company?" Vera asked. "Should I leave?"

"Of course not. Don't worry. Only like-minded people ever come to see me. It will be a friend."

But it wasn't. It was the man who sometimes sold me a bottle of schnapps, a shady guy who dealt in all kinds of black-market goods. He handed me a bottle of liquor and apologized that the price had gone up again. When I went back to my room to fetch the money, an idea struck me: maybe he could get hold of a B.D.M. outfit for Vera. I asked him in and inquired.

"It won't be easy," he said, "but I'll try. It will cost you," he warned as he left.

"It will work," I told Vera, and I was glad to hear her sigh of relief.

Before we went to bed, I dug out a photo album, one that

held many photos of our time together at school. Fifteen years seemed as if they were wiped out when I saw Vera and myself at a school outing. Between us stood Doctor Peach, our German and Latin teacher.

"Look at yourself," Vera said, smiling. "Your pining eyes on your beloved Doctor Peach."

For the first time I heard Vera laugh.

"Yes," I said, laughing too. "I certainly was in love with him."

"Once you even confessed that you were always hoping 'Peachel,' as we called him, would faint, and you and I could carry him out of the classroom. 'I'll pick him up at his head,' you declared, 'and you, Vera, can pick up his feet.'"

We both laughed.

"Remember how ugly Doctor Peach was?" Vera asked.

"Not to me," I replied.

"I know, and I admired you for always speaking up for him. It took courage when all the other girls talked about his unclean fingernails, about a missing button on his jacket, and his bandy legs."

I nodded, remembering back to those years when courage was defined by defending a teacher who wasn't an Adonis.

"And look here!" I said. "Here is Hans Haller. You certainly had a crush on him."

A beautiful blond boy stood between Vera and me. His right arm was around Vera's shoulders. Vera bent over the photograph and looked at it intently.

"Yes," she said. "But it was more than a crush. We loved each other. We even got engaged."

Vera prevented me from turning the page of the album. Then suddenly, she took her forefinger and covered up the figure of Hans.

"What happened?" I asked.

"The inevitable," Vera replied without a hint of bitterness in her voice. "He withdrew when he learned that I was Jewish. It was a great hurt to me at the time. But had he stayed with me, I would have been heartbroken anyhow. A month after we separated, he died in a car accident."

I let Vera sleep far into the morning. Thank goodness there was no air alarm during the night.

After a skimpy breakfast, Vera told me she would like to sell some of her jewelry. She wanted to venture out by herself so as not to involve me.

But I didn't let her. Instead I tried to reach my friend Theo. Theo was exempted from war service. As a journalist, he held a war-essential job at a daily newspaper. It had once been an important liberal paper, but was now a mouthpiece for the Party. He was the nephew of Berlin's cardinal and lived at his uncle's priory in the part of Berlin called Berlin-Center, an older part of the city than the western section where I lived. Some weeks ago, Theo had spoken about a certain rich man he had met. This man's passion was collecting jewelry. But contrary to most people who took great advantage of Jews who *had* to sell their possessions, Theo knew this man was honest and paid appropriate prices for goods offered him. Theo would give us the name and address of this man.

Since my telephone was once again out of order, I decided to go to Theo's place. It was a half-hour walk through powdered glass on the sidewalks and mortar dust in the air. Vera hadn't seen acres of ruins yet. She walked in silence, shaking her head in disbelief. The streets were patrolled by police and S.A. men. They stopped nearly every male. There were only a few who were not under sixteen or over sixty-five in the street. But these were thoroughly checked.

Suddenly Vera stopped and turned ashen. "Look," she said, "there's a middle-aged man who probably is a Jew. He's just walking into this trap."

"If he were a Jew, he wouldn't be here in bright daylight, unless he had gotten himself some Aryan papers," I comforted Vera.

"Should that be the case," Vera said, "and they find out, he'll be executed within twenty-four hours. That's a new law."

We passed the S.A. men as quickly as we could, getting a cheerful Heil Hitler greeting and flirty glances. "Two real German beauties," one of them called. "Yes," the other one confirmed, "and one day they will give beautiful German boys to Führer and Fatherland."

We quickened our pace. "Don't look back," I said to Vera, who wanted to find out what was happening to the middle-aged man. But I did. I saw him being handcuffed and pushed into a black van close by.

Only the housekeeper was at home in the priory. The Herr Doktor would not be back before late afternoon, she told us. She gave me a sheet of paper so I could write a note to him: *Please come to see me as soon as you can. It is urgent. Ilse.*

On our way home, we passed a store with a handmade sign: Jewelry Bought and Sold. It wasn't a jewelry store; most of them had been closed by court order some time ago.

"I have one ring with me in my pocket," Vera said. "Should we go in and ask whether the owner is interested?"

We did. I, not knowing anything about the value of jewelry, was startled to learn how valuable this small ring was. Vera was quite close to selling it, but I was suspicious of the ever-smiling shopowner with the golden Party badge on his lapel.

"Let's wait for Theo," I whispered.

"I have only three marks left," Vera whispered back. "I have to give you some money."

"Nonsense," I said aloud, and the shopkeeper, applying this remark to the offer he had made for the jewelry, turned with a mawkish smile to Vera. "I can add five percent to my offer."

But before a deal could be made, I pulled Vera out of the store. We walked a few blocks and came to a small patisserie. Artificial Honey Tarts—No Coupon Needed! One Portion per Person, announced a large sign.

I suggested we risk this temptation. "But mainly to rest," I added, remembering Vera's swollen feet.

The small café was dimly lit, but the chairs were comfortable. One other table was occupied by two middle-aged ladies.

"They look like schoolteachers," Vera said, and I agreed.

The two small, very small, tarts brought to us did not look bad, but tasted awful. We ate them anyhow. The radio was blasting march music, but changed to the "Horst Wessel Lied" after a while. With the first sound of it the two ladies got up and raised their right arms. Then, one of them, with her left arm, gave us a signal to get up, too. If I had been by myself, I would have remained seated; but, having Vera with me, I did not want any kind of confrontation with these ladies, and I got up. However, I did not raise my arm in the Hitler greeting as Vera, thank goodness, did.

The bill presented to us for these tarts-cum-"Horst-Wessel-Lied" was enormous.

"It did me good anyhow," said Vera, squeezing my hand.

Slowly we walked home, stopping frequently to look at the impoverished window displays. The clothing seemed especially bad. One could see, even without feeling them, how poor the fabrics were. Artificial, all of them.

When we were back in the western part of Berlin, Vera was surprised to see many well-dressed women in the street, young girls and women in elegant fur coats, though it wasn't really fur-coat weather anymore.

"The contrast," Vera said, "to the poor way most women are dressed is astonishing. How is this possible?"

I told her that these girls and women had husbands or boy-friends stationed in Norway or Paris or God knows where. They plundered the country and sent the goods home.

I only became aware of how angry my voice must have sounded when Vera, with infinite tenderness, said, "Don't be so bitter, Ilse. It hurts only you. Not those who deserve to be hurt."

I felt a bit rebuked. Should I be ashamed of myself and my anger?

"How can you be so angelic, Vera?" I asked, ending a long silence.

"I'm not angelic at all. I just try to save my soul."

Vera's equanimity overwhelmed me. But it also upset me a little.

"Your soul is safe," I said. "It's your pretty body we have to save now."

Vera smiled.

Turning into Meinekestrasse, I was surprised and happy when I saw Theo standing in front of my house.

I introduced Vera. Theo in his friendly but flippant way said,

"Now I can see, my dear Ilse, why you wanted me to come so urgently. I had to meet Vera."

It was obvious Theo liked Vera at first glance. I was glad; it would assure his helpfulness.

After I explained Vera's situation, Theo, of his own accord, offered not only to give us the address of the decent rich man but also to take Vera there as soon as possible.

"We can go right now," Theo suggested. But since it would have meant another long walk for Vera, we set a time for the following day.

Vera wanted me to go with her, but I thought it better they went by themselves. Theo picked her up early in the morning, and not till late afternoon did they return. Vera showed me her pocketful of money and told me she had had a wonderful day. Theo had taken her to a museum, to the zoo, and to dinner at the Kaffee Kranzler.

"It was not my doing," Theo interjected, "that it was just cabbage with potatoes. It's one-pot-day today."

"And," Vera said, "for the ring I got nearly twice as much as the shopowner offered yesterday."

Theo and Vera were still telling me about their day when the black marketeer arrived.

"Yes," the man said, "I can get hold of a B.D.M. outfit. You can have it tomorrow if you give me a thousand marks now."

"A thousand marks? A thousand marks!" Theo was indignant and he wanted to bargain.

But Vera quickly reached into her purse and handed over the money. The man, whom I only knew as Paul, left, and Theo scolded us.

"At least you should have given this guy only half the payment now and the rest when he delivers."

"True," Vera said, "but . . ."

I understood her eagerness and her haste. I convinced Theo that we needn't worry. This man, as long as I had known him, had always kept his word.

Theo left a few hours later, promising to come back tomorrow evening to see Vera in her B.D.M. costume.

Vera and I stayed home all day waiting for Paul to come. He didn't. Toward evening Theo arrived.

"Where's the uniform?" were his first words.

We shrugged and shook our heads. Theo did not say it, but "I told you so" was written all over his face.

"You two stay here," I said. "I'll go to Paul's place and find out what has happened."

Though I knew only his first name, I was sure people would guide me to his apartment when I reached the house he had described as the corner house at Lietzenburger and Uhlandstrasse. "Just wall to wall with the post office," he had said.

I found the post office, but at the neighboring corner house nobody had ever heard of anyone named Paul. I knocked on many doors, describing Paul's looks as best I could, but to no success. I felt awful.

As I left the house, the air-raid sirens shrilled, announcing a heavy formation of bombers was on the way. I ran fast, trying to avoid being ordered into a shelter. I wanted to be with Vera, knowing that Theo, who was deathly afraid of bombardments, would surely have left to take shelter in the nearby Zoo bunker.

To my surprise, however, I found the two of them huddled together on my couch. Theo was pale, very pale, and Vera had fear in her eyes, but they smiled when I came in.

We did not hear nor feel much of the attack, though we were aware of wave after wave of bombers passing over us.

"I didn't make it to Paul's house before the alarm sounded," I lied, so as not to dishearten Vera. "But if he doesn't show up during the day, I'll go to see him tomorrow evening."

After the all clear sounded, the radio informed us that Berlin-Center had been heavily hit. The infamous enemy forces, we were told, having no humane feelings for sacred buildings, had obviously made the old cathedral and the adjacent priory their main targets. The cathedral was completely destroyed, and the adjacent buildings in flames.

"Theo!" I exclaimed. "Theo, your uncle!"

Theo sat on the couch, frozen for seconds, then jumped up, touched Vera's cheek briefly, said good-bye, and hurried off.

The following day, again waiting for Paul, we did not dare to leave the house. And again we fled into our past with the help of my photo album. I opened it, and once more we were twelve years old. Vera was always the prettiest in the group photos, though she did not always look happy among all the smiling and laughing girls. Sometimes there was a melancholy expression on her face.

Coming to a certain photo, we both gasped and looked at each other, and finally laughed.

"This is Lotte!" Vera exclaimed. "How do you happen to have a picture of her? She wasn't a close friend of yours."

"I really don't know."

We stopped laughing.

"Poor thing," Vera said.

"Yes, poor thing," I repeated.

And then we tried to put the pieces together.

"Wasn't it you," Vera asked, "who was sent by the principal

to go to Lotte's house and find out why she had not come to school for a whole week?"

"Yes."

"Tell me," Vera said, "I've forgotten how it happened."

"Well," I said, remembering. "When I got to Lotte's house, her mother let me in and answered my question about Lotte by opening the door to Lotte's room. There she sat, in a rocking chair, with a tiny baby in her arms. 'I didn't know you have a baby sister,' I said. Lotte looked down at the baby and her unpretty face became kind of beautiful when she, shyly smiling, said, 'It's *my* baby.'"

We kept looking at Lotte's face.

"I'm ashamed now," I said, "to remember that I left as fast as I could. I didn't know what to say or how to behave. Of course, I was only twelve years old."

"And so was Lotte," Vera put in. "How speechless we were when you came back and told us."

At that time, we didn't know how it could have happened. One week before Lotte gave birth, she had won a gold medal for our school in a swimming contest. Nobody seeing her in a bathing suit had detected her condition. She had always been a bit plump, that was all.

Lotte never returned to our school, and what became of her neither Vera nor I knew.

"Years later," I said, "when I was more grown-up, my mother, who had attended a meeting at the school shortly after this disaster, as the principal called it, told me that Lotte, asked by her mother what the boy had done to her, had answered, 'Oh, nothing much. He just pulled me into a doorway for a couple of minutes and raised my skirt.'"

Vera and I could not take our eyes off Lotte's face. Intrepid and smiling, she stared back at us.

Looking at the album, time passed quickly. It was early afternoon when the doorbell rang. I hoped it would be Paul; but it was Theo.

"Your uncle?" were my first words.

"He is fine. But the cathedral . . ." Theo shook his head.

"Is it gone completely?" Vera asked.

"You must come and see," Theo said.

The closer we got to Berlin-Center the heavier the smoke in the air became. There were row after row of fresh ruins, still smoldering. The dome of the cathedral, which had been a landmark, did not exist anymore. A big area around it was cordoned off, but Theo, showing his card with his priory address on it, was allowed to pass.

"Look," he said, "the priory building is badly damaged, but our living quarters are half all right. No gas, no water, no electricity, of course."

He led us to the cathedral, or rather to the smoldering mass of stones that had been the cathedral.

"Look," Theo said again.

And our minds could not conceive what our eyes saw. In the midst of all the rubble, one column was standing unharmed and erect: Mary with the Christ child in her arms. There were only a few scratches on her bright blue gown.

I can't remember how long we stood and stared, just as motionless as the statue. Not a word was spoken. Finally, Theo took our hands and guided us over heaps of stone and rubble to his place in the priory.

The old housekeeper, also wordless, ushered us to a red plush sofa in a large, dark room and minutes later brought us cups of hot peppermint tea. I think none of us spoke a word until we said good-bye to each other.

Theo added, "Survive." That had become the customary fare-well greeting of the Berliners, replacing the usual Auf Wiedersehn. This time Theo kissed Vera's cheek.

On the way home, Vera told me that yesterday, when she was alone with him, Theo had asked her to marry him.

"And?" I asked when Vera stopped talking.

"Well, Ilse, you know the answer."

"I'm not sure the answer should be no. Your papers don't show you are Jewish, and your looks don't show it either."

But Vera remained quiet, just shaking her head.

After a while Vera said, "I could not do that to Theo. Sooner or later the truth might come out. And besides . . ." Vera took a deep breath. "And besides, I think Theo was just motivated by pity for me."

"I'm sure he likes you, Vera. Likes you very much. I've never seen Theo so attentive and tender before."

"But it isn't love," said Vera, blushing.

"I wouldn't know. Probably this is Theo's way of loving. Want-ing to protect you and do something for you."

But Vera was adamant. "No," she said with finality.

The following day, Vera and I again waited for Paul to show up. But he didn't. In the evening Theo came and declared he would go to Paul's place immediately. I gave him the same de-scription of Paul's house that Paul had given me and let him go. But as soon as he had left my room, I made an excuse to Vera and ran after him. I caught Theo in the corridor and told him what really had happened when I went looking for Paul.

"I don't want Vera to know the truth yet." I persuaded Theo to play along in this sham.

"But for how long?" he asked.

"Well," I said, hesitantly. "There's still some hope Paul will come through, don't you think?"

It seemed fortunate that at that very moment the air-raid sirens wailed again, and Theo and I returned to my room.

"Of course you can't go now," Vera said, and Theo sat down beside her, pulling her head onto his shoulder.

It was not a severe attack, at least not in our area. Once the walls trembled and fine mortar dust drizzled from the ceiling. For a moment, we felt as if we were inside a cloud. We couldn't see the wall facing us, and our throats burned. We started to cough. Seconds later it was quiet again. The all clear had not yet sounded when the doorbell rang. I thought it would be the warden whose job it was to make sure everybody was in the basement shelter, so I didn't answer.

The ringing went on and on.

"I'll go, Ilse," Theo said. "I'll tell him you aren't home."

He went to the door, and a moment later he returned with Paul at his side.

Paul unwrapped the B.D.M. uniform: a simple blue skirt, a white cotton blouse, and a black kerchief held by a leather clasp.

No glamorous silken party dress or wedding gown could have been received with more joy and gratitude. And Paul, as an apology for the delay in delivering the goods, added a bottle of schnapps, for which I thanked him profoundly.

"Well," whispered Theo in my ear, "for this enormous amount of money he could have added two bottles of liquor."

Paul left, and Vera changed into her new costume, as Theo called it.

"It's frightening how convincing she looks," grumbled Theo. "If Vera were a bit older, we could arrange for a Mother's Cross to be pinned on her bosom."

"Being a B.D.M. girl?" I asked.

"Oh, well," mused Theo. "You know the Führer wants as much cannon fodder as he can get. Where it comes from, he doesn't care . . . as long as it's racially pure."

Theo tried hard to lighten the mood we were in. All three of us knew in our hearts that Vera's departure was imminent. And when she said, "Tomorrow or the day after tomorrow," we knew what she meant.

"The day after tomorrow." Theo and I said it in unison.

Vera nodded. Theo frowned. I became teary-eyed and left the room. When the all clear sounded, I decided to leave the two of them alone for a while.

"I want to go and see Fred," I told them. "I'll be back in a couple of hours."

But I did not go to see Fred. Amid the silence of the ruins I walked on and on, searching inside myself for something to give me hope. Hope was what we all lived on. Sometimes it was hard to come by. When it diminished, fear took over. What could I do or say at Vera's departure, I wondered, to give her hope? I didn't know. Could Theo, so much more intelligent and pragmatic, fulfill this wish of mine?

How much longer, I asked myself, could the horror of the Thousand Year Reich continue? In eleven years, most of the German people had not yet understood that their Führer was leading them to ruin and destruction. However, I could not quite give up the hope that Hitler would be assassinated by his own people. But I was called naive for having this hope. Hadn't the attempts to kill him all failed, giving him more power? In the eyes of many, he now seemed indestructible. Protected by providence!

I turned a corner and thought I was dreaming. Out of the ruins a bright, bluish light shot torchlike up into the dark, moonless sky. In a gaping, burned-out window frame dangled the corpse of a hanged man. The scene was unreal—even Bosch-like. I stood and stared.

"A broken gas pipe has caught fire," I heard someone say.

The man who had stopped behind me also seemed over-whelmed by this sight. A minute went by before he asked, "Aren't you afraid? Alone at night in the deserted streets?"

"No," I said and turned to look at him.

His face was illuminated by the flaming torch, which made his dark eyes sparkle and his black hair shine. He was middle-aged, tall, and slim. He spoke with a sharp accent, rolling his r's.

As if trying to deny the macabre scene before us, he continued talking. "I'm Spanish, sent by my government to live in this god-forsaken country to . . . well, I really don't know for what."

"And I'm German," I said. "Condemned to live in this god-forsaken country."

There was an instant understanding between us.

"Where do you live in Spain?" I asked.

"In Madrid."

"A Franco admirer?" I asked.

"Heavens, no," he said. "And you?"

"I'm lost. Completely lost. I hate Hitler, but I love Germany. Germany, the way it used to be."

"I can understand that."

"Do the Spaniards like the Germans?" I asked.

"I do, as long as they aren't Nazis."

"What about German Jews?"

"There are good, and there are bad ones," he said. "Like all of us. I'm a good one."

"A Jew?" I asked.

"No, not really . . . though far back there is some Jewish blood in my family."

My mind raced: Spain . . . Madrid . . . Vera—I acted quickly.

Vera and Theo were startled when, ten minutes later, I introduced José to them. And, as only under certain and blessed circumstances things sometimes come together, we all felt like friends.

A long night of talk began. Questions, answers, and valuable information were shared. José gave Vera names and addresses in the north of Spain where she could stop and spend a night in comfort on her way to Madrid. He also advised her where it would be best and safest for her to cross the Pyrenees. I just watched and listened, feeling elated, a bit like a fairy godmother who had brought good tidings.

It was after three o'clock when José and Theo left. Vera and I, too excited to sleep, kept on talking and planning.

On the day of Vera's departure, she left part of her money and some pieces of jewelry with me. "For later," she said, "if I survive. Will you keep it for me?"

Now, as a B.D.M. girl, Vera could dare to take the trains. We had fabricated a story to make her travel seem justified.

I said farewell to her in my room. It wasn't easy for me to keep a smiling face up to the end. I let Theo take her to the Zoo

Station, but when she left, something of myself went with her.

Theo had done his best to seem cheerful. But when he, after having put Vera on the train, returned to me, he sat for a long time slumped in my chair, motionless and wordless.

Vera and I had agreed she would not send word before she set foot on Spanish soil. And then just a word.

I was anxious and worried. Four long weeks passed, and Theo came by nearly every day. Incessantly we talked about Vera and, depending on the state of mind we were in, we foresaw disaster or success for her adventure.

Then, one morning, her beautiful handwriting on a postcard turned my day into a happy one.

Love

L O V E *?" Christa asked. "Are you still naive enough, Ilse, to take love seriously?"*

"Why not?" I replied.

"Well, aren't you aware that the era we live in is not suited to sentimental feelings like love?"

"I don't agree. I think we need love and tenderness more than ever before to be able to survive unharmed. And I think I am in love."

Christa looked at me with pity.

"For heaven's sake," she said, "if you have the itch, just go to bed with him. But don't tell yourself—or him—you love him."

I realized it had been a mistake to tell Christa about Gerd. But I felt compelled to finish this conversation: "He told me he loves me too."

Christa shook her head and, for just a moment, the prettiness of her face was gone, replaced by an expression of intense disgust.

"It's only sex," she said. "Sex is what all men—and a lot of us women, too—are after. How could it be otherwise? Especially now when nobody knows what the next day, or even the next hour, might bring. Men can be sent to the front, and we can be burned to cinders or lie crushed under the rubble of our houses."

"That's true," I interjected, "but . . ." I could not finish my sentence.

"So," Christa went on, "don't hang your heart on anything.

Least of all on a man. As far as I'm concerned, I have changed my life. This is no time to wait for the man of your dreams. I have learned to enjoy loveless sex, too. Try it!"

I was silent.

"Say something," Christa urged.

But I didn't.

Love, love, love, I thought. I could not depreciate love and, instead, value and respect sex—loveless sex.

A scene I had witnessed recently—a desperate scene—came to my mind. I did not tell Christa what I had seen, but in my inner eye, I saw it again. I had taken a friend to catch a train. The railroad station was crowded with people, most of them young soldiers on their way to the Russian front. The eastbound train was on its track already. However, its departure was delayed because of a bombardment on the outskirts of the city. Most of the soldiers were seen off by their wives or girlfriends. There were tears and embraces. There was heartrending sobbing and . . . there was sex. Wild, unabashed sex. On the benches. On the littered concrete floor. People stepped over the writhing, moaning couples as if they were stones on a rocky path.

One lonely young soldier who had watched an intertwined, copulating couple at his feet suddenly stepped close to us, put his arm around my waist, and tried to kiss me.

I pushed him away.

"No," I said, firmly but kindly.

That was enough to make him blush.

"Forgive me," he whispered and went off.

Later, on my way home through devastated streets, I wondered: Should I have let the young soldier kiss me? Wasn't it cruel of me to push him away?

A kiss—just one kiss—might have meant love to him.

Otto

I WOKE UP after a bad night. One of those nights when, in sleepless hours, you wonder about yourself. What had happened to the young and naive woman who, six years ago, had fled her hometown and come to Berlin full of hope and curiosity: hope to put her past behind her and become an artist; curiosity about what the big city would have to offer. However, the ongoing war with its increasing deprivations had made normal life impossible. And what had happened, step by step, to art was more than sad, it was disastrous.

I remembered walking through the exhibition of Degenerate Art, where not only the masters of German expressionism but also the French impressionists and post-impressionists were categorized as degenerate. I walked through this exhibition and heard the laughter and scornful remarks of the masses filing through. I remembered how the Nazis judged jazz. They said it was nothing but a noise intended to poison the ears and the minds of the civilized Germanic race, aiming "to unroot the racial instinct of the people and tear down the borders of their blood." Bombastic nonsense like this boomed out of the loudspeakers.

The same was true, the Nazis maintained, of most foreign literature. Bookstores were not allowed to sell Russian, American, British, and other foreign writers. All Jewish authors, German or otherwise, were banned, as was every living writer whose Weltanschauung did not coincide with the ideology of the Nazis. What,

I asked myself, were the opinions of the censors based on? I couldn't understand. I only knew one thing, and I knew it more by instinct than reason: thoughts and attitudes like these should not only be resisted, they had to be fought.

But what could I do? I would have liked to join a group of organized resisters and do something really worthwhile. It was rumored there were several such groups in Berlin. But never had I actually heard of one, nor had anyone among my anti-Nazi friends had contact with such a group. But I did not give up hope of finding one, and eventually I did.

It happened in a very unexpected way: in my landlady's kitchen. Up on a ladder, painting the ceiling, was a man. He was slim, small, and agile, with a fine-featured head and quick, observant eyes. He did not look like a housepainter to me, though he introduced himself as one when I entered the kitchen to prepare my breakfast.

It was the middle of July 1944. On D day, June 6, the Allies had invaded northwest Europe. On the eastern front, the German army was in steady retreat; the Russians were deep into Poland and nearing the German border. But the German morning news reported that "our Führer is full of optimism," that we all had "nerves of iron" and that "the situation on the eastern front presents no problem." I was fuming. I could not hold back. I had to let my anger out.

"I agree with you," the man on the ladder said. "But, my Fräulein, you are very careless, talking like that."

"So are you, agreeing with me," I snapped back.

"No," he said, "I'm not. Frau Lasker told me you were all right and I believe her. You would not be living with a half-Jewish woman otherwise."

Now the door was open to a lively exchange of our thoughts

and feelings. He told me he had been a teacher but was expelled because he was a member of the Communist Party. He was Jewish also, but the Nazis had not found out yet. And because he saw what the future would bring, even before Jews had to wear the yellow Star of David, he and his half-Jewish wife went underground.

"I can just barely make a living by doing odd jobs, which like-minded people offer me," he said.

"Shall I give you the address of a friend who would like his room painted?" I asked.

"Oh, yes, that helps," he said warmly. "Thank you. That helps a lot."

"That's nothing," I said. "I wish I could *really* help. Help in a big way. Do something to hasten the downfall of Hitler and his regime."

At my words, he came down from his ladder and put himself in front of me. Looking me in the eyes, he asked, "Do you really mean what you say?"

I assured him I did.

He told me he belonged to a well-organized group of resisters, and if I passed a test necessary for acceptance to his group, he would arrange for me to join.

The following day, he came by with a wad of envelopes. The test consisted of my dropping these envelopes in designated mailboxes at designated times.

"The content of the envelopes?" I asked.

"That's not for you to know. They just want to find out how reliable you are."

"Who are 'they'?"

"That," he answered, "you will be told later."

It took two full days, during which I crisscrossed Berlin from one suburb to another, before I had all the letters deposited. This done, I got another dozen envelopes. Painstakingly I posted them, instantly destroying the timetables I was given. This went on for two more weeks. It did not satisfy me. Not that I had hoped to become a Mata Hari, but this kind of job, I felt, any idiot could have done.

"Patience," my sponsor, whom I knew only by his first name, Otto, admonished. "Patience. We cannot take chances. But there is one thing you can do now. You can name another reliable person, someone you know well, who will join us, too, and for whom you will be the contact person. Can you think of somebody?"

"I can."

"Good," Otto said. He explained that his group used the chain system as their working method. "Only three people: you—I— and your friend will ever know each other in person."

"Why is that?" I asked.

"It is a good safeguard. Never more than three people are endangered should there be a weak link in the chain. Do you understand?"

I nodded.

"And now, since you've proven reliable, I'll tell you for whom you are working: the Communist Party." He stopped, looked at me, and asked, "Is that understood?"

I nodded.

"We are the only hope for the future. Capitalism, democracy, even socialism have all failed. Only we can bring justice and equality to the world."

He looked at me again, and again I nodded.

"So you agree to work for us?"

"Yes, I do."

"Good," he said. "But before I give you important work to do, you will have to promise, under oath, that you will join the party and work for it as soon as this war and Hitler's Reich are finished.

"Tell me you will," he urged when I did not answer immediately. "Promise."

But I was quiet. I was not prepared for this demand. I had been an unpolitical person before the outrageous evil of Hitler and his regime became obvious. I was willing to contribute what little I could to help bring this nightmare to an end, but I was not willing to commit myself to any kind of political activity after the end of the war.

I told Otto my feelings.

He was very disappointed. He told me that, under these circumstances, he could not accept my services.

His voice was cool and sober now. His smile was forced when he, saying good-bye, added, "Let's stay friends anyhow."

My response was warm and honest. "Yes, I hope so. And if I can be of help to you and your wife, in personal affairs, just let me know."

Nine months passed, during which I did not see Otto.

Then, when the Russians and the Germans were fighting in the streets of the eastern part of Berlin, he and his wife stood at my door, asking whether they could spend a night.

They were in terrible shape, especially Klara, Otto's wife, who was hollow-eyed and trembling, hardly able to speak.

It was Otto who told me what had happened.

They had been waiting impatiently for the arrival of the Russians, their liberators, and had stepped out of their hiding place when they heard Russian voices in the street. With a white band around their arms they proudly presented their precious Communist Party cards. They had, at great risk, kept them all these years.

"Just for this occasion," Otto said.

Then the Russian soldier, obviously not comprehending what he held in his hand, spat on the cards, threw them on the ground, trampled on them, and shouted: "Nasi! Nasi! Nasi!"

I was enraged and speechless.

"But that isn't all," Otto continued.

Klara buried her face in her hands.

"The Russian dragged Klara to a nearby burned-out house and . . . raped her."

I began to weep. And it was Klara who comforted me: "It's over now," she said. "I survived."

I shared some bread and sausage with them, let them sleep in my bed, and asked Frau Lasker to let me sleep on the sofa in her living room.

When I entered my room the next morning, they were gone. A note explained that they had wanted to leave before daybreak. They blessed me and thanked me over and over for a good night's sleep.

A postscript said: *Please, do not think unkindly about Russia. These are just soldiers . . . the Russian people are different. Don't close your heart to them.*

"No," I said out loud. "No—I won't."

Hunger

———

ONCE UPON *a time—and it seems ages ago—when the words* I am hungry *meant, I'm ready to eat again, I did not know what hunger was. I did not know that hunger was a mind-killer, a growling beast inside you demanding to be fed and occupying all your thoughts.*

But now I know: the beast's growling is steady. But every so often the beast howls and convulses. It is then that all discipline forsakes me and greedily I devour the last piece of dry bread, which should not have been eaten before tomorrow.

I regret it immediately, because the beast is not satiated. It keeps on howling.

I get frantic and try to silence the beast inside me by reaching for a book.

"Who, if I cried, would hear me among the angelic orders?"

One of my favorite poems. It used to elate me. Today I stop after the first line. Cry? Cry for what? A slice of bread? Maybe a slice of bread with a touch of butter on it? Or a little ham? Or a bit of cheese?

I had heard of people who had killed for a piece of bread. I wonder: could that be true? Where did they find the strength for so violent an act? Hunger reduced me to sheer apathy.

Slumped in my chair, strawberries suddenly appear on a screen in my mind. I see the strawberry patch in the garden of my childhood. I hear the maid whipping the cream in the kitchen. The sparkling cut-glass bowl holding the mountain of red strawberries stands in the center of the table, which is covered with white linen. The peaked whitish whipped cream and a basket of biscuits stand nearby. Mother, Grandmother, and I sit down and . . .

Stop! I order myself.

Stop it—don't torture yourself. You will not die of hunger. You will lose another pound or two, but starvation is not your destiny.

At least not yet.

Hajo

I REMEMBER CLEARLY: It all began with a ring of the
telephone on Monday, August 21, 1944. For once the shrillness of
the ring did not seem ugly to me. It was a pleasure. Also a surprise!
The phone had been silent for almost a week after a heavy air raid
had hit Berlin. It will be good news, I thought. It will be one of
my good friends.

It was Fred.

"I'm glad your phone works again, Ilse." He spoke with great
agitation. I missed his usual cheerful greeting. Without waiting
for a word from me, he continued: "Ilse, are you alone?"

Again he did not wait for my reply.

"I'm coming over right now. Will be there in fifteen minutes.
Should somebody come to see you, you *must* send him away. Bye-
bye." He hung up.

Fifteen minutes later, I heard a knock at the hall door. The
doorbell had been out of order for weeks. I went to open the door
and was surprised: Fred was not alone.

A young man I had never seen before was with him.

Quickly Fred, the stranger close behind him, rushed through
the dimly lit hall into my room. I closed the door behind me and
followed.

"Is your landlady home?" Fred inquired.

"I'm not sure."

"Go and make sure," he commanded.

"But, Fred, it's not important whether she's here or not. Even if she catches a word or two of our conversation, she is on our side: a fervent anti-Nazi. I've told you before, she's half-Jewish."

"I know, I know," said Fred impatiently, "but just the same I would feel much better if she did not know we are here."

I went out into the hall and called for Frau Lasker. No answer. I knocked at the several doors leading to her rooms. No answer. Returning to my room, I found Fred nervously pacing the floor. The stranger, however, was stretched out on my couch smoking a cigarette.

He hadn't been introduced to me yet: Fred did that now.

"Ilse, this is Hajo. A friend of a friend of mine. He is in trouble, severe trouble. He has reason to believe a *Fahndung*, a search, is out on him. By the Gestapo."

"Why?" I wanted to know. "What for?"

"Well, Hajo has spoken frankly, which means slanderously, about Hitler to a colleague he trusted. Another colleague, an anti-Nazi and on Hajo's side, has now informed him that the trusted colleague is a provocateur and has denounced Hajo, which will certainly bring the Gestapo to Hajo's door." Fred stopped, took a deep breath, and, with a rueful smile he added: "To make things worse . . . Hajo is half-Jewish."

"Is he?" I asked, looking at Hajo, whose face was turned to the wall.

"Up to now, though," said Fred, "thanks to the fact that Hajo is an excellent chemist and since there is a great shortage in this profession, he had a job in a pharmacy supplying the high command of our army. Through great carelessness, however, he has endangered not only his position but also his life. He has to go underground immediately." Fred stopped, looked at me, and asked, "Do you have a question, Ilse?"

"No," I said, "go on."

I tried to see Hajo's face, but since he was still lying down, turned to the wall, I only got a glimpse of his half profile and the pitch-black hair on his head. He was smoking and seemed never to take his eyes off his cigarette. Once in a while, he raised his left hand, free of the cigarette, held it at arm's length, and thoroughly studied his long, well-manicured fingernails. I had the impression he didn't care what was going on. As if it didn't concern him at all.

"Well," Fred continued, "we need your help, Ilse. Until we find a permanent hiding place for Hajo, you must let him stay with you. He will be safe here."

"Why will he be safe here?" I asked.

"No trail will lead to you since you did not know him before today. Nor do you know anybody belonging to his circle of friends." Fred paused, looked at me, and asked, "What do you say, Ilse? You certainly can't say no."

"Yes," I said, "I can't say no." But fearful thoughts went through my mind.

A sigh of relief from Fred.

Not the slightest reaction from Hajo.

"It won't be easy though," I said. "You know I have only this one room."

"It doesn't matter," said Fred. "Put pillows from your couch on the floor, and Hajo will be satisfied."

He looked at Hajo for approval, but Hajo was scrutinizing his fingernails again and did not even turn his head.

"Besides," Fred continued, "it will be for a very short time: one or two nights. Hajo's friends will come up with a solution. I'm going to see one of them now. I'll be back soon."

With that Fred walked over to Hajo, slapped him on the shoulder, and said, "That's it. Behave yourself."

He embraced me hastily and left.

Now I was alone with this strange stranger. What was I to do? I couldn't think of anything to say. In my mind he registered as an intruder. I felt helpless and upset. The silence that followed seemed endless, and I wished I were a child again and could scream, stamp my feet, and cry: *Get out!*

Hajo turned his head and looked at me. For the first time, I saw his full face: narrow, pale, with dark, glinting eyes under black, bushy eyebrows; a long nose over a small, dark mustache, which partly covered thin lips that seemed to be frozen in a permanent, cynical smile.

And then he spoke for the first time: "You do not seem to like me."

"I don't like the situation," I replied.

"So—why do you agree to this arrangement?" he asked.

I searched my mind for a plausible answer. "Because . . . ," I said, "because an enemy of my enemies, the Nazis, I consider to be a friend."

"Well, then, let's be friends," said Hajo. "And to seal this friendship, let's have a drink."

He pulled a crystal flask from his pocket, screwed off the silver lid, and offered it to me.

Without hesitation, even greedily, I took one sip—two sips— three sips. I handed the flask back to Hajo. It was strong hard liquor. I felt its effect immediately.

"Half empty," Hajo said, grinning.

"Oh, I'm sorry," I apologized.

"Never mind," he said. "When it gets dark, I'll go and get more."

He looked around my room.

"They're nice," he said, pointing to the large Matisse and Renoir reproductions pinned to the wall.

"Well," I said, "not much furniture left. I sent most of it to my parents' house in Silesia."

"Smart," he said, "but why didn't you send yourself, too?"

Before I could answer, he asked, "Do you intend to survive the Thousand Year Reich?"

"I guess so," I said.

"Well," he said, "I *definitely* do! It can't take too long anymore until it's all over. The Allies are already close to Paris and are pushing toward the Rhine."

Hajo got up and walked to the farthest corner of my room, where my Queen Anne secretary once stood. It was empty now.

"Would this be a good spot for me to sleep?" he asked.

"All right," I said. "And I'll hang a blanket over my easel and move it close to the corner. That will give you some privacy."

"Good idea," he said, and immediately we arranged his sleeping nook. Six of my large couch pillows became a small mattress.

Hajo lay down to try it out. He laughed and said, "It must do."

"Do you have food in the house?" he next wanted to know.

"Very little," I told him. "There are still three days before the new ration cards."

"Forget it," he said, reaching into his pocket and pulling out a wad of food coupons. "Can you go and shop a little?" he asked, handing me coupons for bread, butter, and meat.

"Where did you get so many?"

"Don't ask questions," he said, putting a wad of paper money in my hand.

"But I can't leave now," I declared. "I'll have to let Fred in. He promised to be back soon."

It took hours, however, until Fred returned. I could see immediately that things had not gone well, although Fred tried to cover up with a nervous sort of laughter.

"Nobody was home at any of the three addresses you gave me," he said to Hajo.

"Well, try later, at night," Hajo suggested. "Or early tomorrow morning."

Fred nodded good-naturedly. Now I could go and shop.

Hajo invited Fred to stay for a meal. "No coupons needed," he added with a smile of largess.

When I came back with full bags, we all went to the kitchen. Fred, fond of cooking and good at it, turned the meat into a stew, spiced it nicely, and each of us had a large portion.

Back in my room, Fred was amused to see the sleeping nook we had arranged for Hajo.

"Oh," he said, "I almost forgot. I went to your apartment, Hajo, and asked Emmy to give me a pair of your pajamas."

"Did you tell her where I am?" Hajo wanted to know.

"Of course she asked, but I told her it would be better if she didn't know. I assured her that, for the time being, you are well taken care of."

Hajo nodded.

Fred left. And again I was, and uncomfortably so, alone with Hajo. I was glad when he said he would go out as soon as it got dark.

"Isn't that risky?" I asked.

"Ah, now the little lady worries about me," he said. "Maybe she likes me after all."

Spontaneously I shook my head, then regretted it and forced myself to smile. "Well, of course I worry. Tell me more about what happened."

"It's better you don't know the details. Just know they are out to get me. I must run for my life."

I didn't press any further, just asked again whether it was wise for him to go out.

"It's dark now," Hajo said, "and wise or not wise, we need liquor."

"I don't need any liquor," I said emphatically.

"Oh, yes, you do," was Hajo's response. He went to the door and said, "Maybe you could give me a key so I needn't knock coming back."

"I have no second key," I said.

"You don't need your key because you won't go out," Hajo persisted.

I gave him my key. The moment he left, however, I could not believe what had happened. Why did I let him control my life? I ran after him to get my key back. When I reached the street, I did not know whether he had turned right or left. It also was much too dark already. Back at my door, a shock: the door had fallen shut after my hasty and thoughtless departure. I was locked out. There wasn't anything I could do but wait for Hajo's or my landlady's return.

Angry and miserable, I paced back and forth for half an hour.

Then Frau Lasker arrived, surprised to find me shivering in front of the door.

"Come to my room," she said. "I'll fix you a hot cup of tea."

I liked my landlady, a kind and considerate woman, much older than I. She had told me that her husband, a Jew, had left

Germany two years before, and she was hoping she would be able to follow him to Spain. But up to now, it had been impossible for her to get a visa.

I accepted her offer of tea gratefully. I also was eager to tell her what had happened in the past few hours.

She understood and smiled. "I hope it doesn't get you in trouble" was all she said.

I went back to my room, and soon Hajo returned.

Out of a brown paper bag he took three bottles of hard liquor and asked me to fetch two glasses, which he filled to the brim. Then he handed me my key.

"You can keep it now," he said in a benevolent voice that vexed me. But when he went on to say, "I had a copy made for myself," I got really quite angry.

However, I drowned my anger in a large sip of schnapps. After the second glass I asked, "Tell me, Hajo, who is Emmy, the person who gave Fred your pajamas?"

"Oh, her," he said with a shrug. "She's just a girl."

"You live with this girl?"

"We happen to share an apartment. That's all."

"Tell me about her."

"I don't like to talk about her. Besides, don't be so nosy."

A little rage visited me. I took another swallow of schnapps. Be patient, I told myself. He is hunted. Hunted by the monsters who rule Germany.

As an evasion, I turned on my radio. Luckily a radio play was on, which canceled any further conversation. Every once in a while Hajo threw out a sharp, cynical remark about the sentimental plot. Often it was a witty remark and made me laugh.

At eleven, when the play was over, I said I wanted to sleep

and asked Hajo to go and change in the bathroom. I was in bed when he returned and, as was my habit, reading before falling asleep.

"Lucky you," Hajo said. "I have no reading light in my voluptuous lair."

"Too bad," I said. "I hope you won't be condemned to another night of such misery."

"Thanks for your compassion," Hajo snapped back, throwing himself with a sigh on his bed of cushions.

Anger welled up inside me again. I had to admit to myself that I had disliked Hajo on first sight. Had he not been a persecuted person I would not have covered my dislike with politeness. But he *was*, and so, again, I suppressed my feelings and only thought, poor hunted creature.

A few minutes later, my voice tender now, I said, "Good night, Hajo."

His response was, to my surprise, a lullaby. He hummed Brahms's Lullaby.

The following day was a nervous day of waiting. Fred came and went and telephoned, a hundred times it seemed to me, to report about his unsuccessful efforts to get in touch with one or another of Hajo's friends.

Hajo himself took it all surprisingly calmly. "It's all right," he said. "I feel fine being a prisoner in Ilse's little lair. Besides," he added, "we have enough schnapps for several more days."

"But something has to be done," Fred said.

"Yes," I said and suggested as a start that we change Hajo's looks.

"How?" asked Fred.

"The color of his hair," I said. "Get me peroxide, very strong peroxide, and I'll bleach Hajo's hair."

"Of course," Fred said.

"Poor me," grunted Hajo, running his fingers through his thick black hair. "But," he said, grinning, "I'm curious to see what I'll look like as a blond Aryan."

Fred went out and bought a tall bottle of peroxide, and I went to work immediately. I doused Hajo's hair generously with the liquid and expected an instant result. Years before, in a silly attack of vanity, I had wanted to lighten my ash-blond hair, and I was startled, even horrified, to observe how quickly my hair color changed to a much too light shade of blond. I had washed the peroxide out as quickly as I could.

With Hajo it was different: nothing, absolutely nothing, happened to his hair. We waited and waited; and instead of washing the peroxide out after an hour, I poured another heavy dose on Hajo's head. He was a funny sight sitting under the large white sheet I had thrown over his shouldes. Tentlike, it covered his whole body.

One of his hands, sticking out of the tent, held a hand mirror with which he tried to watch the oncoming of his blondness.

Fred laughed.

I, however, didn't feel like laughing. I wanted a quick and drastic change in Hajo, hoping it would relieve me of my obligation to hide him. Hours went by. We had to interrupt our task to eat a bite and, as Hajo insisted, have drinks.

I, who wasn't used to drinking hard liquor during the day, got a bit dizzy. But the schnapps also brought a welcome lightheartedness, so that at the end of the day I too could laugh about our unsuccessful endeavor.

"Patience," Fred said, "patience. Tomorrow is another day."

"Yes," I said, "and where will Hajo be tomorrow?"

"Darling Ilse," Hajo said, "you wouldn't want me to leave before your ingenious idea to turn me into a German Siegfried is realized, would you?"

"Of course she wouldn't," Fred said. "Ilse is a responsible person. We can rely on her. And besides," he said, turning to me, "we haven't found another place for Hajo yet."

Harrowing days followed with daily and nightly bombardments. Hajo, of course, never went to a shelter. The days were filled mainly by dousing peroxide on Hajo's hair. On the third day his hair took on a slightly orange shine. On the fourth day it became a brassy orange. It looked very unnatural. His eyebrows were still black and so was his mustache.

"Shave it off," ordered Fred, who arrived in the afternoon and was pleased when he saw Hajo's red hair.

"This must be celebrated," declared Hajo, and when he found out there was only a trifle of schnapps left in one bottle, he went out to get more.

This was my chance to talk privately to Fred. I asked him who Emmy was.

"Didn't Hajo tell you? It's the girl he's been living with the last few years. She is extremely worried about him."

"Are they just friends?" I wanted to know.

Fred laughed. "Hajo might want you to believe so, but Emmy is certainly very much in love with him. Of course, he cannot go back now."

"I understand that, Fred, but someone must be found to shelter Hajo. I can't go on hiding him forever."

"I'll do what I can, Ilse, but I know you wouldn't want to put him out on the street."

We couldn't continue: Hajo was back.

"Success, success," he announced gleefully, putting three bottles of schnapps on the table. Immediately he uncorked one bottle and filled three glasses.

"I don't want any," I said.

Hajo emptied his glass in one swallow. Then he drank my glass, too, and poured himself still more. Fred was in a drinking mood, too. I felt a rage building up inside me when I saw how quickly both of them guzzled down one glass after another.

I said, "I'm going out."

"Why so angry?" asked Hajo. "Why do you want to leave?"

"Because," I said, "I don't want to watch the two of you get drunk. Besides, I haven't been out of the house for several days."

"There isn't much to see out there but ruins," Hajo said. "Ruins and the smoldering debris from last night's bombardment. Be happy you can stay inside with two good friends."

"I'm going to see a good friend," I replied, emphasizing the word *good*. I threw an angry glance at both of them.

I left, and when I turned into the Kurfürstendamm I saw there was a new gap in the row of gutted houses. And, indeed, the debris was still smoldering, filling the air with thick smoke. I took the kerchief from my neck and tied it over my nose and mouth, which made breathing a bit easier. I decided to go and see Christa, who lived a few blocks away.

It was getting dark now. Here and there a figure slipped by, and here and there sparks, like fireflies, floated through the darkness. When I reached Christa's house, the air-raid sirens sounded. I met her hurrying downstairs, lugging bundles and a suitcase to the basement. Christa knew I never went to a shelter, but she wanted me to follow her. I tried to persuade her to let me stay in her apartment.

"I can't stand being herded together with all those people," I said. "Nazis, most of them. I can't stand their hysterical voices, cursing the 'air gangsters,' using the same vocabulary that is blasted at them day and night over the radio."

Christa did not give in. "Never mind," she said, "it's the law." And she insisted on my following her.

I knew that Christa was deathly afraid of air raids. For a long time she had been talking of leaving Berlin. But the prospect of spending her time in her parents' parsonage in Pomerania seemed to delay her departure from week to week.

We reached the shelter. It was crowded already. We had to squeeze ourselves between some people huddled on a wooden bench. Christa reached for my hand and held on to it tightly. In her free hand she clasped a Bible—a brand-new one it seemed.

I had come to Christa to talk about Hajo and the awful situation I was in. I hoped she might know a way out for me. She, a fervent anti-Nazi too, had many trustworthy friends. Maybe one of them could help to hide Hajo. But, of course, it was not possible to talk with so many people within earshot. We sat without speaking. And as Christa's trembling hand held on to mine, the years of our friendship passed in rapid succession through my mind.

I had met Christa shortly after my arrival in Berlin about six years before. I came from a small provincial town to this big, often called "sinful" city. I had been told—or better, warned—I would be meeting "all kinds of people" there. "All kinds of people," I assumed, meant, people different from me. I was curious and eager to meet them. Christa was one of them. The daughter of a pastor in Pomerania, she frequently complained about the stern upbringing she had endured. She was an artist. A painter, she told me.

However, I never saw a painting on the large easel that served her as a clotheshorse. She talked a lot about Picasso and Matisse and many other famous artists. She had even spent a year in Paris, and I was awed by that. She was petite and pretty, bright and witty, and she startled me, who was naive and shy, with her self-confidence and her Weltanschauung. Also with her own kind of morality, which, especially regarding sex, deviated from the moral code I had grown up with. She talked freely and frequently about her several lovers. And when I asked, "All at the same time?" she replied, "Why not? No harm in that. Making love is better than making war."

Then she went on to tell me that if she had a daughter, she would bring her up to become a courtesan. "Men," she explained, seeing me frown, "men who steadily chase women and try to get them to bed should pay for what they want from them."

Timidly I said, "But I believe in love."

Christa laughed and put her arm around my shoulder, and with unexpected tenderness said, "Of course you do. You are a romantic, Ilse, and I like you for it." Quickly she changed the subject, and then it was a pleasure to talk with her. I had just discovered some American writers who were, due to a Nazi edict, on the list of forbidden authors: Faulkner, Wolfe, Wilder, and Hemingway. Christa had read them all, and I was happy to share with her my enthusiasm for their writing.

But now, here in the shelter, her fear had silenced her. Once or twice I tried to talk to her. No response. Her grip on my hand loosened when the all clear sounded.

"I'm sorry I can't ask you to come up and stay," she said. She had a date, she explained.

I walked home slowly, dreading having to face the drunken

Hajo. I should have asked Christa to let me spend the night in her place, I thought, but it was too late now. I walked far out of my way to delay my homecoming. Finally, turning into my street, I saw bright orange-colored smoke covering several houses in my block. Yellow flames shot out of the smoke, illuminating the night sky.

My heart pounded. Was my house on fire? I quickened my pace, and soon I could see the burning house was at the end of the block, several houses removed from mine. Crying and scream-ing people milled in the street. But no fire brigade and no firemen were in sight. There were probably many more houses on fire, and not all fires could be attended to. Some of them just had to burn themselves out.

Arriving home, I let myself into the hall and, listening, I stood in front of my door. I heard nothing. Maybe Hajo and Fred had gone out. Or, better still, Hajo was already asleep. I opened the door quietly.

My room was dark, but I heard Hajo snoring. Good, I thought, I needn't talk to him. I shut the door, went to the bathroom, and changed into my pajamas. Quietly I entered my room. Without turning on the light, I tiptoed to my couch, intending not to make up my bed, but just to sleep under a blanket.

I let myself down—and bumped into something. A scream! Then a thrashing movement. By now I was screaming, too, and struggling to free myself from a tight embrace. With great effort, I reached for my night lamp and turned it on. The light fell on Hajo's twitching face. He did not seem fully awake yet.

He let go of me, threw his arms in the air, and cried, "Help! Help me! Help!"

I got up quickly and looked down on Hajo, who slowly came

to his senses. Recognizing me, he put his hands over his face and muttered, "Ilse, where have you been for such a long time? I dreamed you'd never come back."

"Well, here I am," I said. "Back."

Hajo got up, too. He reached for my hands. In a kind of frenzy he kissed them. "Forgive me, Ilse. Please forgive me."

"All right," I said, "all right." I didn't know what else to say. I felt defeated. I felt helpless and sorry for him. And I was tired.

Hajo dragged himself to his "lair" behind my easel and went to sleep.

Waking up the next morning, I found a note from Hajo beside my bed.

Ilse,

I have left. For good. I know I am a burden to you and (well, I have to admit it now!) since I have fallen in love with you, I cannot bear the thought of making you unhappy. Whatever destiny has in store for me—survival or death—I will accept it. Thank you for the days of shelter and care you so generously bestowed on me. I felt safe and protected.

Good-bye,

Hajo

This piece of paper lay in my hand with the weight of a rock. I did not know what to make of it. Was it serious? Was it a joke? I was glad when Fred arrived, earlier than usual, to, as he put it, check up on Hajo.

I showed him Hajo's note.

Fred burst out laughing. "Melodrama," he said, "sheer melodrama. I bet you Hajo will be back before the day is over."

"But I don't want him back."

"I know that, Ilse, and I feel sorry for you. But for the time being it can't be helped. However, I'm thinking about a different solution."

Before Fred could explain, I heard the hall door being unlocked, and a moment later the door to my room opened.

There stood Hajo.

Not Fred nor I nor Hajo said a word. The uncomfortable silence ended when Hajo put several breakfast rolls and half a pound of butter on the table.

"And," Hajo said, pulling a jar out of his pocket, "raspberry jam. For you, Ilse. Your favorite."

Speechless, I left the room. Listlessly I sat in the kitchen, for how long I didn't know, until Fred came to fetch me.

"Ilse, I had a serious talk with Hajo. Since we can't find anybody here to hide him, he, after many arguments, accepted my plan. He'll leave Berlin and go to the Rhineland. That is, *if* we can come up with the necessary preparations."

"Why the Rhineland?" I wanted to know.

"For two very good reasons. First, the Rhineland will, much sooner than Berlin, fall into the hands of the Americans. Paris is liberated already and the Allies are heading for the Rhine. And second, Hajo comes from the Rhineland. He says he has many friends there, and, best of all, a sister married to an Aryan scientist working in a high position for the government."

"That's fine," I interrupted, "but how will Hajo get to the Rhineland?"

"That's where we need your help again, Ilse."

"I'll do anything I can," I assured Fred. "What am I supposed to do?"

"We need some papers for Hajo. Papers from the Army High Command that order him to travel to the Rhineland."

"Yes," I said, "I see. And since I told you once I know someone—"

"A forger," Fred interjected.

"An expert," I corrected Fred. "An expert in making different kinds of documents—"

"Yes," Fred interrupted again. "And since you know this person, you can probably get the necessary papers made."

I didn't respond immediately. Though the thought of being rid of Hajo was more than tempting, I wondered: Could I burden my friend, Oskar, with such a demand?

"I'll try," I said after a while. "I certainly will try."

Ten days later Hajo was ready to leave: reddish blond by now and equipped with papers carrying the stamps of the *Oberkommando der Wehrmacht* that ordered him to attend meetings at I. G. Farben in Düsseldorf and Cologne. In his navy blue business suit and carrying a brown leather briefcase, he looked respectable and official.

Fred and I walked Hajo to the Zoo Station. We had arranged to arrive just a couple of minutes before the train was to leave in order to make the farewell short and sober.

"Good luck, Hajo," I said, and I meant it.

Hajo squeezed himself into the train overcrowded with soldiers. He turned back to look at us.

"For heaven's sake! I hope you aren't going to cry," said Fred when Hajo's eyes got moist.

"I'll miss you," said Hajo, his eyes fixed on me. "I'll miss you very much."

And then, thank goodness, the train began to move.

My room, without Hajo, seemed paradise. I sat down and felt as if an angel were sitting on my shoulder. Then I tried to remember: what had my days been like before Hajo's intrusion? It seemed so long ago. For the moment, however, I wanted nothing more than to relax and enjoy the stillness of my room. A reproduction of the *Odalisque*, a painting by Matisse, hanging on the wall in front of me, gave me pleasure and comfort. Yes, comfort! Didn't it, or she, suggest there was more to life than the daily struggle for survival? That it was worthwhile to stay alive until this war came to an end? But *was* the end of the war really near? And would I then be able to devote my life to serious painting?

To avoid further thinking about unanswerable questions, I reached for a book, hoping to lose myself in it. But after reading a few pages, I put it down. Nothing I read had reached my mind. I was not yet free of Hajo. I followed the train carrying him away. I wondered if he would pass the inspections, customary on trains nowadays. And would his sister be willing to endanger herself and her husband by hiding Hajo, a fugitive?

Remorse began to gnaw at me, and I asked myself: Had I done enough for Hajo? Would I have done *more* had I not disliked him so? Suddenly I could not stand the quietude of my room. Hastily I slipped into a jacket and ran out into the street.

But the street was no comfort either. By now I had gotten used to the lingering smoke and the smell of gas in the air, the glass from the broken windowpanes crunching under my feet. What I had not gotten used to was the fear in the ashen faces of the passersby. Most of them were women. One seldom saw a male between sixteen and sixty on the street. And most of the children had been evacuated long ago.

Aimlessly I walked about.

After a while I decided to go to the nearby KaDeWe department store. I needed a frame for one of my paintings. A few days before Hajo's arrival, I had finished a very large one: a blooming alpine meadow in front of a mountain range. It was colorful and pompous enough to fetch a good price from one of those people for whom art does not exist and for whom a scene, arousing a desire to be there, is reason enough to buy such a painting.

For a long time, frames had not been available. But there was no shortage of certain kinds of well-framed pictures that were for sale. They were portraits of Adolf Hitler. I had already bought several, removed the portrait—gleefully cutting up Hitler's face —and had inserted my painting in the frame.

As so often nowadays, the current in the store was off. Instead of riding the elevator, I had to walk six flights up to the art department where a whole row of Hitlers stared at me. Most of them were reproductions of paintings, and in most of them Hitler was dressed in his ugly brown uniform. There were photos, too. Photos showing the Führer smilingly accepting a nosegay from a little girl. Or he was sitting on the terrace of his mountain retreat, the Eagle's Nest, in the Bavarian Alps, his shepherd dog Blondi at his side.

I had seen them all before, but today there was a new painting: Hitler, full figure, nearly life-size, in a dazzling white uniform, standing on the top of a mountain, surveying conquered land. The picture, a reproduction, had an impressive frame which I felt would raise the price of my painting considerably.

"How much?" I asked the salesman approaching me.

The price was surprisingly low, which, as the salesman explained to me, it should be. "Every German," he said, "regardless of his economic situation, should be able to afford a portrait of Hitler, the savior of our German race."

Then, suddenly, the salesman looked at me intently, and a mawkish smile spread over his face.

"The Fräulein must truly love our Führer," he said with an approving nod. "I remember having sold you two other Hitler pictures a few weeks ago. Of course," he added, "it's nice to have one in every room."

"Well," I said, "that's true. But my need goes beyond that. I'm an interior decorator and of course . . ." I didn't need to finish the sentence; the salesman nodded understandingly.

"The painting is very big," I said. "Let me see whether I can carry it." I lifted it, but it was difficult.

"What a pity," said the salesman, "that we have no home delivery anymore—you know, the shortage of personnel. Everybody has a war-essential job nowadays." The permanent saccharine smile on his face made room for a sorrowful frown. "But," he said a second later, "I myself could bring the painting to your place in the evening after I'm through with work."

By now he had moved so close to me that I felt his breath on my cheek. Brusquely I turned my back. "Thank you," I said, "just bring it to the cashier."

I acknowledged his good-bye and his "hope to see you again" with a cool smile, waited until the picture was wrapped, and left.

It wasn't easy to lug this weighty package. Every so often I had to stop and rest. Thank goodness I had not very far to go. But just the same, with every step the bundle seemed to gain weight. By the time I reached home, I was quite worn out. And hungry, too. There was one leftover cold potato from yesterday's lunch. Greedily I ate it before I unwrapped my treasure.

The picture was too large for the easel. I had to lean it against it. Looking at this horror, I suddenly had an idea. It was a nice, wicked idea. It made me smile. Snipping this picture in little pieces did not seem enough. I decided this stupendous one should be put to better use. It should undergo a grand mutilation. And my friends should participate in the execution of it.

I invited Fred, the Kleine König, Christa, and Theo to a party. When asked what the occasion was, I did not answer.

The following day, before my friends arrived, I prepared my room. First, I covered the painting with a white bed sheet. I put out little jars of poster colors and brushes. I set a few candles, only three, in the far corners of the room, so that the room would be dimly lit. Then I positioned a lamp on the wall opposite the painting to be turned on only at the appropriate moment. I still had a full bottle of schnapps—Hajo's bequest.

The first one to arrive was the Kleine König. As always he had his long red scarf wound three times around his neck. I had, literally, to unwrap him.

"We haven't had an air raid yet today," he said meekly.

"Good," I said, "isn't it?"

"Well, that means we will have one soon," he said with a fearful face.

"Remember," I tried to console him, "the largest and safest of all public bunkers is at the Zoo Station. Just minutes from here."

His forced smile did not erase the fear in his eyes.

The next to arrive was Christa. Since she, too, was frightened ·

of bombardments, I immediately reassured her: "You and König can run to the Zoo bunker as soon as the alarm sounds."

Theo was the next one to arrive. He also was afraid of bombardments. However, he was able, at least most of the time, to cover it up.

With a raised fist and a grunted Sieg Heil he greeted us. "It's clear," he announced, "we'll win the war. Our fat-bellied Marshal of the Air Force, Hermann Goering, was able to hold back the American *and* the British air gangsters all day today."

I laughed. But Christa said, "The day is not over yet."

"Nonsense," quipped Theo, "the day is over! The night is still to come. And let's hope it will be a still night."

König, in an attempt to be humorous too, began to sing *"Stille Nacht, Heilige Nacht."* But his effort misfired; nobody laughed.

We hadn't entered my room yet; we were still in the hall waiting for Fred. He arrived and was astonished to find us milling about the hall, glasses of schnapps in our hands.

"Will it be a Hitler pogrom?" he asked. "Or is it rather to celebrate Hajo's departure?"

"Well," I said, "maybe it's both."

I led them into my room. "Sit down," I commanded, "and nobody is allowed to remove the sheet from the painting leaning against the easel. I'll do that after we have finished our drinks."

"Aaah," said Theo. "Our Ilse will unveil one of her masterpieces. Let's guess what it will be!"

"Well," mused Christa, "Ilse is so fond of Goebbels, our Minister of Culture. She could have been inspired to do a painting of him, clubfoot included."

"No, no," protested Theo. "Ilse is a romantic. A pompous wedding would be more to her liking. Maybe she has painted Air

Marshal Goering and his statuesque Karin eating from golden plates at their wedding party in Karin Hall."

König only shrugged. "I'm curious" was all he said.

Fred hadn't said anything yet. Now he walked toward the easel. "No, no," I protested, holding him back.

"I won't touch it," he said. "I only want to smell it." Then he performed a grotesque little dance around the easel. With his hands locked behind his back he sniffed the sheet, and in a portentous tone of voice he announced, "I know! It's a portrait of Hajo!"

"Who is Hajo?" Christa asked, astonished.

And Fred replied, "He is one of Ilse's well-kept secrets. Her unrequited love."

Everybody looked at me. I shook my head vehemently, then laughed out loud. And though nobody knew what it was all about, they joined me in laughing. We finished our drinks.

"Now!" I said and switched on the light which spotlighted the covered-up picture. Slowly I walked toward it while Theo softly whistled "Here Comes the Bride" The short moment of utter silence after I had removed the sheet ended in a burst of laughter.

I poured another drink for all of us. We clicked glasses.

"To his death!" shouted Theo, stepping close to the painting and punching Hitler in the face.

"Not so fast," I said. "We will first transform him. Let's go to work."

I opened the paint jars, took a brush, and with quick strokes I painted wide black stripes on Hitler's white uniform. Then I handed the brush to Christa. She set the landscape surrounding Hitler in flames. Theo put a chain on Hitler's feet, and König put chains on his wrists. The brush was returned to me again, and I changed Hitler's billed cap into a prisoner's headwear. In a mixture of laughter and wrath, we exhorted and urged one another on to do more and more to the picture. Finally there was nothing left of the original painting but Hitler's face, which we had not touched at all.

Satisfied with our work, we calmed down. There was a bit left in Hajo's bottle, and we enjoyed it while gazing at the transformed picture.

Suddenly I had an idea. "Later," I suggested, "when it's pitch-dark outside and the streets are empty, we could carry our Führer to the center of town and set him up against a lamppost across from the Reichschancellery."

I expected enthusiastic approval, but it was not forthcoming. Instead I was declared reckless, foolish, even crazy.

"Would you like to have us all killed?" asked Christa accusingly.

I pretended to pout for a moment, but then reached for my brush again, dipped it deep into the black paint, and put a large vulture on Hitler's shoulder. That brought instant and enthusiastic approval.

"Let's slaughter him now," Fred said.

"Go get a knife," Christa ordered.

I went to the kitchen.

At that moment the air sirens shrilled. Seconds later, returning to my room, I found it empty. My friends had hurried away without saying good-bye.

I sat down, my back turned to the Hitler painting. I could hear the droning of the planes and the thud of what must have been the explosion of bombs rather far away. The next explosion, however, was closer and made my walls tremble ever so slightly. I held my breath and listened. No more explosions followed, but wave after wave of planes passed overhead, obviously heading for another part of the city.

I remained seated, waiting for the all clear, which did not come for a long time.

All at once I became aware that my right hand still clutched the big kitchen knife. The sight of it caused an unexpected horror inside me. I let it drop to the floor. I was afraid of myself. Could I really kill Hitler if I had the opportunity? One voice inside me said yes; another one said no. Quietly I began to weep. I did not like myself. I did not trust myself. And, worst of all, I did not feel like myself.

It was an hour before the all clear sounded. I knew my friends would not come back for the real assault on Hitler, stabbing him and cutting him to little pieces. I understood. They wanted to be home before the subways and streetcars stopped running, which they did rather early now.

But I felt restless. I wanted to talk to somebody. I thought of Anna Dach, who lived just a few blocks away from me. I had only known her for a couple of months. I liked her, though she was not a close friend. But her outspoken spite for Hitler made me feel comfortable with her. And, to be honest, there also was another attraction: whenever I visited her, a large basket filled with fruits, cheeses, pumpernickel, even coffee and chocolates, was standing on her table. And though these were unheard-of rarities and luxuries that could not be found in the shops anymore, Anna was eager to share them. She would even force things into my pockets when I left.

"How do you get them?" I asked.

"My fiancé sends them." After a pause, she added, "He has connections."

"Tell me about your fiancé."

"There isn't much to tell," she said. "I love him. He is a kind and intelligent man. However, before I found that out, I fell in love with his looks. He is tall, blond, and blue-eyed."

I waited for her to go on, but she didn't. Oh, my God, I thought. He, of course, is a high Nazi official. Probably he belongs to the S.S., thanks to his super-German looks. That's why he has access to things unattainable by us common mortals, who have to live on sparingly rationed food.

"I would like to meet your fiancé," I said.

Anna nodded. "Yes, that would be nice. I'm sure you would like him."

"Then let's set a date," I suggested.

"That's not so easy," said Anna. "He travels a lot. I see him very seldom nowadays."

I couldn't suppress my gnawing suspicion any longer. "Is your fiancé a member of the Party?" I asked.

"Heavens, no," Anna protested. "The extreme opposite is the case."

"What does that mean?" I asked.

But I got no answer. "Let's talk about something else, Ilse, please."

After this I did not inquire about her fiancé anymore. Once or twice I invited her to visit me, but she declined. "I'd rather stay close to the telephone," she explained. "He might call."

So I visited her. And always there were generous presents from her fiancé on the table. And always Anna shared them.

Now, walking through the dark, deserted streets, my eyes smarting from the smoke in the air, I was looking forward to seeing Anna but also hoping for an apple or a bite of cheese.

Anna answered my knock immediately and said she was happy to see me. But her red-rimmed, swollen eyes contradicted her words.

"Anna, what's the matter?" I asked, putting my arm around her shoulders.

"Nothing," she said, avoiding my eyes. "Nothing. Come in."

We entered her living room and sat down side by side on her sofa.

"Look," she said and gestured at the empty table. "Look, no fruit."

Though I was a bit disappointed, I shrugged and said, "So . . . probably you'll get some tomorrow."

"No," she said.

"How can you be so sure about that?" I asked.

Anna's eyes widened as tears came. Suddenly she leaned her head against my shoulder and sobbed uncontrollably.

"What is it, Anna?" I asked. "What has happened?"

Instead of answering, Anna pulled a letter out of her pocket, wrinkled from having been read over and over. She handed it to me.

"Read it," she said, handing me the letter, which was written in a small, elegant hand.

Anna, my dear love,

This is to say good-bye to you. For months and months—it is nearly a year already—we have not seen each other. How much I missed you I was never able to put into words in my many letters to you. At times when I needed you most, I had to stay away from you. I could not endanger your life, too. It gave me some pleasure to be able to send you if not spiritual then physical nourishment.

This, too, is over now. Within the very next days, I will be on the transport. Good-bye, my beloved. My love for you will only die with me.

Your Walter

There was an addition at the bottom of the page. In extremely small and shaky letters it said: *A comfort—the door to suicide is always open.*

"Walter is a Jew," I whispered.

"Yes," said Anna, "he is."

I did not mind at all that the air sirens sounded again. It gave me a chance to ask Anna whether I could spend the night on her sofa. I didn't want her to be alone. She agreed immediately and seemed pleased.

We slept deep into the morning. Since Anna's larder was completely empty, we went shopping. For an hour we had to stand in a line only to find out, when our turn came, that the jam we had coupons for was sold out. So was the margarine. A dry slice of bread was our breakfast, and after it we decided to go for a walk.

It was a lovely day. The mild September sun was not held back by a layer of smoke and dust, since the western part of the city had not had a heavy bombardment recently. We strolled along the Landwehrkanal, an arm of the river Spree flowing through Berlin. In prewar times it had carried many barges. Now debris floated on its murky water. The banks were lined with chestnut trees, many of them mutilated. But some of their beautiful shiny brown fruits with their velvety whitish spots were strewn on the ground. We picked some up just for the pleasure of rolling them in our hands.

"A pity they aren't edible," Anna said.

"I heard they are ground and added to our malt coffee," I told her.

Though I would have liked to hear more about Anna's fiancé, I tried my best to prevent her from thinking about him. I told her how I had arranged for the "Hitler assassination" the day before, and how the final execution had not taken place because of the air alarm.

"But," I said laughing, "it *will* take place soon."

Anna did not join me in laughter. She became extremely serious and asked, "Are you telling me the picture is still in your room?"

"Of course," I replied. "There was no time to cut it up because all my friends had hurried to the public bunker when the air-raid sirens howled. They will come back another day for the stabbing, and you, Anna, are invited, too."

Anna stopped walking. She put herself in front of me.

"Ilse," she said, alarm in her voice, "how can you be so reckless? So careless? It would cost you your life if the wrong person should see this painting." When I tried to interrupt her, she continued, "One never knows nowadays under what unforeseen circumstances a stranger could get into your room."

"I turned the painting against the wall," I said defensively.

"That's not enough, my dear. You must go home immediately and destroy it. I would go with you, but I have an appointment I must keep."

Before we separated, I had to promise Anna to follow her advice. I was miserable on the way home. I wanted so badly for the execution party to take place. I felt I sometimes had to do something reckless. I felt I sometimes needed to let out the accumulated anger and despair. I wasn't quite sure if I would keep my promise to Anna. Who, for heaven's sake, would enter my room in my absence?

When I arrived home, Frau Lasker met me in the hall. "You have a visitor," she announced with a strained smile.

I opened the door to my room and found Hajo stretched out on my couch.

"Oh, n-o-o!" I exclaimed, letting myself fall into a chair.

"Oh, yes!" Hajo echoed my tone.

He got up and approached me with outstretched hands.

"Oh, no," I said again, burying my face in my hands.

Hajo put his hands on my shoulders.

"Didn't you get to your sister?" I asked, pushing his hands away. "What went wrong?"

"Nothing," he said, "really nothing. I made it to my sister all right. Only . . ."

"Only what?" I asked, irritated.

"Only—I found out that living away from you isn't worth living at all."

"Hajo," I burst out, "don't dramatize! Don't talk nonsense!"

"Love is not nonsense," Hajo insisted.

"Love has nothing to do with all this," I said firmly. "Not for a second did I ever feel anything close to love for you, Hajo, and you know it. All I was willing to do was help, so you would not be caught."

"Well," asked Hajo, "isn't that a kind of love?"

"Absolutely not! I would do that for anybody, friend or not."

By now I was so furious, I lost all control. I screamed so loudly at Hajo that it caused Frau Lasker to open the door and enter my room.

I was beating Hajo's chest with my fists.

"Come," she said, pulling me away.

She took my hands, and willingly I followed her to her living room.

"Sit down, darling," she said and put her hand on my still-trembling one. "Let's talk."

She, of course, had been aware of Hajo's previous presence in my room. She had not objected. She understood. I had told her how we had arranged for Hajo to get on a train to the Rhineland. "I'm glad for you he's gone" had been her response. Now I told her the reason Hajo had given me to explain his return.

"And I can't stand him," I said. "I really can't. If he were not a fugitive, a person in great danger, I would not want to have anything to do with him. Let alone have him stay in my room."

"Poor child," Frau Lasker sympathized. "What will you do now? Will you be strong enough to put him out?"

"Of course not," I said with a bitter laugh. "I'm really trapped between my feelings for Hajo and my feelings against the Nazis."

"Well, maybe I can offer a little help to ease your situation," my landlady said soothingly. "Hajo can sleep here in my living room until another solution is found. The sofa will be comfortable enough. Besides, it will not inconvenience me at all because I'll be away for a couple of weeks. What do you say?"

I flung my arms around her neck. "Thank you, thank you, thank you!"

Hajo was not delighted when I told him about the new arrangement.

"There is no other way," I insisted.

"We will see," he said. "Maybe you'll change your mind when you see this."

Out of his pocket he took a small, blue leather box.

"For you," he said. And with an annoyingly smug smile, he opened it.

Inside, on red velvet, were a bracelet and a ring, both decorated with a dazzling number of diamonds and rubies.

I just glanced at them and quickly turned my back.

"Take it away," I said.

"No," said Hajo. "Look at them, Ilse. Please, look. They're family heirlooms."

I turned. "How did you get them?" I asked.

"From my sister," said Hajo. A sly smile moved over his face. "I need to sell them; I need the money to survive. That's what I told her. But it isn't true. What it really is, is an engagement present for you, Ilse."

I was struck dumb. And horrified.

"You're insane, Hajo," I stammered. "Completely insane."

I said it over and over. Hajo remained calm.

"I'll be patient and wait," he said. "We have to wait until this mess is over anyhow, to get married. By then I think you'll be ready to marry me."

"Never," I burst out. "Never!"

"If that is true," Hajo said under his breath, "if that is true, I'll kill myself."

And then, with a measured gesture and striking an attitude as if he were the center of attention on a lit-up stage, he reached in his pocket, pulled out a revolver, and fired a shot at the ceiling.

The sound was deafening. I stood paralyzed—rooted to the ground.

"That's just to show you," he said.

I had hardly recovered when I heard loud knocking at the door in the hall. At first I couldn't bring myself to answer, but the knocking became so vehement that I went and opened the door. The couple living in the apartment above mine were standing there looking concerned and bewildered.

"We heard a shot," the man said.

"What has happened?" asked his wife. "Are you all right?"

I pulled myself together. "Yes, I am." And, forcing a smile, I said, "It was only the popping of a bottle of champagne."

The man and his wife looked at each other, shook their heads, and without saying good-bye turned their backs and walked upstairs.

I did not return to my room. From Frau Lasker's telephone, I called Fred. After I had told him of Hajo's return, he agreed to meet me in half an hour at a bench in the Zoologischer Garten. When I arrived he was already waiting for me. After I had told him all that had happened during the last hour, he promised that he would—more than ever before—try to find another hiding place for Hajo.

"First, however, we must find out what kind of a manhunt for Hajo is in progress," Fred said. "There are different degrees of intensity, depending on the importance of the fugitive," he informed me. "And again, it is you, Ilse, who can help with that."

"But Fred," I said, "will you understand that I'm not convinced anymore that Hajo is worth all our effort, worth the danger we bring onto ourselves?"

Fred nodded.

"Imagine," I went on, "he thought he could buy my affection with diamonds! Jewels he got in a very underhanded way from his sister."

"You're right, Ilse, you are. But let me ask you this—and answer with a simple yes or no: Are you ready and willing to push Hajo out and let him fall into the hands of our enemies? Which would mean his certain death."

"Fred," I said, "you know the answer if you put it like that. But then," I added, "it might not come to that at all. Hajo is a sly fox. I'm rather sure he will somehow get by without our help."

"Maybe, maybe not," Fred said and continued, "I think our decision to throw Hajo out or not should depend on the degree of the seriousness of the search for him."

I agreed.

"Remember the girl you told me about?" Fred asked. "The bar girl, I mean. She works at a nightclub on the Kurfürstendamm. And I know this place is frequented by the Gestapo and the S.S. Maybe she could help to get some information."

"Perhaps," I said. "She took a liking to me after she had made sure I was a Hitler hater." And I told Fred she even had confided in me, with obvious pride, that she slept with Gestapo and S.S. men. She got them drunk, she said, and they got talkative and careless. And then she drew all kinds of information out of them. She had boasted of having helped several men avoid being arrested.

"That's it," said Fred. "We must get her interested in Hajo and set her on his trail."

Fred went home with me to face Hajo and tell him about our plan.

Hajo, who had discovered the Hitler picture, stood in front of it when we entered the room.

Before either of us could say a word, Hajo, with his cynical, malicious smile, said, "Congratulations, Ilse! I see during my absence you've become a Hitler devotee."

Fred behaved as if he hadn't heard the remark. He told Hajo that we would try to find out what kind of warrant was out on him.

Hajo just shrugged and, very casually, said, "If you wish." Then he turned to me. With simulated concern he said, "I think, Ilse, you should not shelter two criminals in your room. One will have to go."

Before Fred could interfere, Hajo again pulled out his revolver and fired a shot into Hitler's face.

"You are a madman!" Fred said furiously. "You really are. Though you are right in this case." And pointing to the Hitler painting, he said, "He must go!"

Quickly we went to work, cutting the painting to pieces and shoving them into a large envelope.

"I'll get rid of this," Fred promised. "I have a friend with a stove in his studio."

Without paying much attention to Hajo, Fred left, promising to pick me up at ten o'clock that night.

What followed wasn't really easy for me. I disliked going to the swanky nightclub on the Kurfürstendamm, which was always swarming with Gestapo and S.S. men. But I went.

When Fred and I entered the club, we saw Frau Koper sitting at the bar. A tall S.S. officer was standing beside her, his arms around her waist. He was swaying and seemed to be holding on to her for support. When Frau Koper saw me, she winked and untangled herself from the S.S. man. He nearly fell after she had freed herself. But she steadied him, put both his arms on the bar counter, and bent his head down until it came to rest on his arms. She whispered something in his ear and left him to join Fred and me.

"Is there a quiet corner where we can talk for a few minutes?" I asked.

"Of course," she said and led us to a small service room in the back. "You understand—I can't stay away long. My boss would be furious."

"We'll make it short," I promised, but before I began to talk, she wanted to know who Fred was.

"One of us," I assured her, and Fred received a strong hand-shake and a warm smile from Frau Koper. She really was a cute little person: sparkling, dark eyes; a mass of brown, curly hair piled up extremely high on her head ("It makes me look a bit taller," she had told me on our first meeting); and a high, twittering, lively voice. What had brought her to this "profession" I did not know. My kind of upbringing would have required me to look down on her or, at least, feel sorry for her. But I could not help liking her from the moment we met. And besides, she truly was one of us: a fervent anti-Nazi.

We stood close together in the small room where boxes, bottles, brooms, and other paraphernalia were stored.

"Shoot," said Frau Koper.

"We need your help," I began. "A friend of ours believes a search by the Gestapo is out for him. Right now I'm hiding him. But to protect him we must know for sure whether—and if so, how serious—a search for him is in progress. Do you think you could find out?"

"How lucky," Frau Koper said radiantly.

It seemed to me a strange reaction.

"How lucky," she repeated, "because the drunken guy you saw standing beside me at the bar is just the right person to have information about such cases. I'll sober him up a bit and take him home with me. Tell me your friend's name and why he thinks there is a warrant out for him."

Fred told Frau Koper what he knew about Hajo's dangerous situation, caused by his careless talk to a colleague who turned out to be a provocateur.

"Come back tomorrow. I'll do my best," Frau Koper said and guided us out to the street.

Eagerly I waited to see Frau Koper again. And again Fred went with me the following evening. We did not see Frau Koper immediately. We found a table in a dimly lit corner. The two drinks we had ordered were a watered-down concoction that tasted awful. The din, the smoke, the chatter, and the loud music made me feel quite uncomfortable. Most of the customers were in uniform, the black S.S. uniform dominating. I was relieved when Frau Koper finally joined us.

The first thing she did was to take a sip from my glass. She shuddered, grimaced, took both our drinks, and carried them to the bartender. A moment later she returned with two fresh glasses.

"Taste these," she said.

"All the difference," Fred said.

"It's a shame," Frau Koper complained, "what they dare to offer customers like you who are not regulars."

"Well," said Fred, "we might become regulars if—"

"Wouldn't that be splendid," Frau Koper interjected. "Some *nice* people instead of all these creepy, uniformed men." And after a pause, she added, "Some of whom I'm not even sure are men."

Then, hastily, because the club owner was keeping an eye on her, she told us that not before tomorrow would her "private eye," as she called the S.S. officer, be able to give her the wanted information.

Another twenty-four hours of waiting in anxiety. I spent most of the day bleaching Hajo's hair again. It had begun to show a suspicious darkness at the roots, especially at the part. It was an extremely unpleasant job for me. Now, even more than before, I abhorred the physical closeness it required. But I knew I had to do it.

There was, thanks to Frau Lasker's generosity, a slight improvement in the situation compared to the first days Hajo had spent with me. He now slept on the sofa in my landlady's living room, which was next to my room. The connecting door was blocked off on both sides by furniture.

Fred did his best to unburden me by spending many hours of the day with Hajo. Eagerly we listened to the reports of the progress the Allies had made on the western front. They were—after they had liberated Paris on August 25—getting closer and closer to the Rhineland. Bitterly I thought how much sooner Hajo would have been safe had he stayed there.

At night Fred and I went to see Frau Koper again. Yes, she had gotten some information: There was a first-degree search out for Hajo which, should he not be found after a fortnight, would be intensified to a second-degree search. Should this also fail, the local search in Berlin would be extended to a national one.

"It's not good news," Frau Koper said gravely. "But I'm glad I could supply it. Should you want more help, well, you know where to find me."

Suddenly I thought of something I had not thought of, nor discussed with Fred, before. I didn't quite know how to go about it, but I felt we should offer to compensate Frau Koper for her efforts.

Clumsily, and being aware of my clumsiness, I said, "It's so kind of you, Frau Koper, to help us so promptly. How much do we owe you for your effort?"

Frau Koper looked aghast. Then she broke out laughing. "My

dears! What nonsense! Don't you know that our dearly beloved S.S. man paid a lot of money for the privilege of spending the night with me?"

Her frankness was refreshing. Fred and I joined in Frau Koper's laughter, thanked her warmly, and left.

Hajo was not at home when we got back.

"Probably he's out to get more schnapps," I grumbled. "He drinks so much and gets terribly obnoxious. I can hardly tame his aggressiveness." I was close to tears.

Fred paced the room nervously.

"Ilse," he said, "it's all my fault. I brought this upon you. Of course, I thought it wouldn't go on for so long. A night or two I said, remember? Besides, I didn't know Hajo well. Had I known him as I know him now, I would not have approached you at all. Ilse, I am truly, terribly sorry."

"Don't," I comforted. "I know life is not a bed of roses. Sometimes one has to endure misery. I'll be patient. I promise I'll not throw Hajo out until we find another place for him to hide."

"But now," Fred said, "after what we have heard from Frau Koper, we—that is mainly you, Ilse—have to be more careful. And, most important, prepared."

"Prepared for what?" I asked.

"Well, I don't want to scare you unnecessarily, Ilse, but it is not impossible, though not very likely, that the Gestapo will find their way to you."

I tried to hide how shocked and frightened I was.

"I guess you know their routine?"

I shook my head.

"They come at the break of day to the suspect's house," Fred informed me. "And we must have a plan. You and Hajo must have a dress rehearsal as soon as possible. It's fortunate that this apartment is at ground level. A jump of no more than three or four feet out the window, and Hajo can escape should the hangmen come."

At that moment Hajo arrived. His unconcerned grin and the way he dumped three bottles of schnapps on the table made me flush with anger. But he did not even notice. Slightly drunk already, he walked up to me and tried to kiss me.

"Stop that nonsense," commanded Fred.

"What nonsense?" Hajo asked. And, faked emotion in his voice, he turned to Fred, saying, "I love that girl."

Fred shook his head angrily. "Sit down, Hajo," he ordered. "We have to talk. The situation is very serious now. I have not only to think of how to protect you, but also, and more important, how to protect Ilse. She is in great danger, too."

Then Fred told Hajo what we had just learned from Frau Koper.

"Nonsense," Hajo snapped. "I'll outfox them. And should they come too close to me . . . well . . ." And with that, he pulled his revolver out of his hip pocket. Fred tried to snatch it away from Hajo, but didn't succeed. With a victorious smile, Hajo returned it to his pocket and sat down.

For a while we all sat in uncomfortable silence.

Then I began thinking out loud. "My room," I said, "is the closest to the entrance door in the hall. Hajo is sleeping next door in Frau Lasker's living room."

"That is an awful arrangement," interjected Hajo. "I don't like it at all."

Fred gave him a stern, warning look.

"So," I went on, "should there be a knock at the door in the early morning hours, I would immediately wake up Hajo. Your clothes, Hajo," I said, turning to him, "must from now on always be close to your bed so you can get dressed quickly and jump out of the window fast. The little garden of the hospital in which you will land will give you good cover. You'll be able to run through the hospital gate into Joachimstalerstrasse, which runs parallel to our street."

"So far so good," Fred approved. "What next?"

"I'll go to the hall door and tell whoever it is—"

"You better first ask who it is," Fred interjected.

"All right, I will. And I'll tell them I need a few minutes to make myself presentable."

"Good," said Fred again. "By then Hajo is many blocks away."

"And then?" Hajo asked. "What then?"

"Well," said Fred, "further I cannot plan. And do not even want to think any further."

Before Fred left, we all went to check the windows in Frau Lasker's room. We made sure they opened easily and silently. We even made Hajo jump out the window—it was easy—and helped him get back in. It upset me that Hajo never stopped grinning and wisecracking as if the whole thing were nothing but a lark.

Our planning and rehearsing had not taken place too soon. Only two days later, I was awakened by knocks at the door. I came out of a deep sleep. I jumped out of my bed, and for several seconds I felt without ground under my feet. The clock said five-thirty. The knocking got louder. I slipped into my robe and headed for Hajo's room. However, the knocking became so vehement that I felt, in order not to arouse suspicion, I should go and answer it first. Through a peephole in the door, I saw two young men in gray trenchcoats, carrying leather briefcases.

"Yes," I said, without opening the door, "what is it?"

"Oh, nothing," replied one man, "just the police. Please open up."

"I will," I said, sounding as eager as I could. "But I must first get into something. I'm in Eve's costume—that's the way I sleep. Give me a minute or two."

I dashed to Hajo, shook him hard, and whispered, "That's it, Hajo. Get up and out. Fast!"

"All right," he grunted, without opening his eyes, "all right."

I shook him harder, pinched his nose, and twisted one of his ears. Precious seconds were lost. Finally he sat up and rubbed his eyes.

"That's it, Hajo! They are here. Get out! Fast!" I took his trousers and jacket from the floor, shoved them into his hands and left, shutting the door.

Then I hurried to the hall door. Two tall, blond men greeted me with a smile.

"It's a bit early," one of them apologized, "but we have to do our duty. May we come in?"

I let them enter the hall. Then I opened the door to my room. They entered, looked around and, still smiling, nodded approval at what they saw. A large painting of sunflowers was standing on my easel.

"Ah," the one who had introduced himself as Officer Miller said, "the Fräulein loves sunflowers, too."

"Do you?" I asked.

"I do," he replied, "though I had thought of Van Gogh when I said that. He has painted many sunflowers."

"He always goes for culture," said the other young man in a belittling tone. He smiled, but his smile did not make his face look friendly.

"Yes, yes," said Officer Miller, "if the war had not come and forced me to serve my Führer and the Fatherland, I would have studied art."

"Would you like to see more of my paintings?" I asked, seeing an opportunity to extend the conversation before they declared the reason for their visit.

"Very much so," said Officer Miller, while his companion nervously checked his wristwatch.

"Sit down then," I urged, and while I was pulling out more paintings from my shelves, I held my breath. Anxiously I listened for any sound that might be coming from the room next door. Thank goodness, nothing. Hajo obviously had succeeded in dressing very quietly. I was, however, waiting to hear the thud when he jumped to the ground. I could not be sure: was he out already or not?

In any case, I fought for time. I entertained the intruders with my paintings and some chitchat about art. But my heart was pounding. Was I good enough an actress to cover that up and seem unconcerned?

Finally Officer Miller changed the subject.

"Tell me, my Fräulein, does anybody else live in this apartment besides your landlady and you?"

"No, nobody does."

"Well, we have reason to believe somebody does."

"How is that possible?" I asked. "If my landlady had someone living with her, I certainly would know. The apartment is small. We would bump into each other in the hall or the kitchen, which we share."

Officer Miller shook his head, fixing his eyes on me, but still smiling his saccharine smile.

"I guess we have to search the apartment," he said.

"You're welcome to do so," I said, smiling too. "However, my landlady is out of town, and she always locks her rooms when she's away," I lied. "But, of course, I think you have the authority to break the locks on her doors."

"Indeed we do," Officer Miller assured me, and for the first time they showed me their cards of identification.

I was so upset and worried, I felt as if I might faint at any moment. I could not even read what the cards said. The fat swastika, however, and the official stamps beside their photographs were enough to convince me of their authenticity.

Where I took the strength from I do not know, but with a gesture toward my door I said, "Please, go and look."

To my surprise, however, neither Officer Miller nor his companion got up. Instead Officer Miller asked where I had studied art and whether I was happy with what I was doing. He didn't wait for an answer; he shivered, hugged his shoulders, and said, "It's cold here. Don't you freeze?"

I made an effort to laugh. "Who doesn't?" I asked. "With the shortage of fuel . . ."

"Yes, yes," Officer Miller said gloomily. "This war is awful. It will soon be over. Don't you think so?"

I did not know what to do. Should I nod approval? Was he setting a trap for me? I didn't answer.

Instead I said, "You know what? I'll brew a cup of tea for us. I have a few real tea leaves left."

Officer Miller followed me to the kitchen. Wordlessly he watched me brewing the tea. When we returned to my room, Miller's companion was pulling out more of my paintings from the shelves. Was he looking for something? Was this a search?

But all he said was, "You are a fine painter, Fräulein."

I thanked him and handed him a cup of steaming tea. I even had a few lumps of sugar to offer.

Both men drank their tea with pleasure. Their attitude had changed. They seemed relaxed now.

When the tea was finished, Officer Miller declared, "We have to leave now. Thank you, my Fräulein, for your kind hospitality."

I showed them out, but before saying good-bye, Officer Miller turned to me, shook both my hands and said, "You must admit, my dear Fräulein, the Gestapo is not as bad as its reputation."

"I didn't know you had a bad reputation," I said. "I enjoyed your company. Come back anytime."

I opened the door, let them out, and shut the door behind them.

By now I was at the end of my strength, of my acting ability, of my courage. I threw myself on the couch, trembling. After I had recovered a bit, I went to Hajo's room to check the state he had left it in. I also would have to close the window. I entered and saw the crumpled mass of blankets on the sofa.

I pulled them off and—my heart nearly stopped!—found Hajo under them. Deeply asleep. Snoring.

For a moment I was speechless, even paralyzed. Then I shook him brutally awake, and a rage overcame me. Something inside me broke. My pity, my compassion, my empathy were gone and replaced by a healthy feeling of self-preservation.

"Out," I said. First quietly, then sternly, then loudly. "Out!" I screamed over and over again. "Get out, Hajo! And I never want to see you again!"

I threw his jacket and trousers at his head, dragged his blankets off him, and left the room.

Minutes later Hajo came to my room. I pulled myself together. After all, I had to tell him what had happened while he peacefully slept.

I did. Matter-of-factly, suppressing my anger.

I finished by saying, "This is the end, Hajo. There is nothing you can say that will change my mind. I will not hate you nor wish you evil. But from now on, I'll think of myself and protect myself instead of you. I will get dressed now and leave, and when I come back in an hour, I want neither you nor anything belonging to you in my place. Good-bye and good luck."

I pushed Hajo out of my room, got dressed, and left. I went to see Fred, who was surprised to see me so early in the morning.

"You did the right thing," he said after he had listened attentively to what I told him. "And I don't want you to feel guilty, whatever might happen to Hajo."

These were the words I needed to hear. With gratitude and relief I started to weep. Fred let me cry for a while.

When I stopped, he asked, "How are you feeling now? Tell me honestly. You are rid of Hajo now; he is out of your life. And how I wish he were out of your thoughts, too."

"That isn't the case yet," I said. "All I feel right now is apathy. A blessed kind of feeling compared to the concern and anxiety of the last few weeks."

And that was as close to the truth as I could come. A catharsis had taken place. I felt free and had strength again to face all the other difficulties that life brought daily during those hard, hard months as the war drew to its end.

Hajo never returned. Neither Fred nor I heard from or about him. We didn't even make an effort to find out.

However, Hajo survived.

But not until after the war did I see him again. He seemed unchanged. Only his cynicism, his sarcasm, his disregard for any kind of regime was now focused on the occupation powers in Berlin. Mainly the Americans and the Russians were now the target of his scorn.

Was I surprised? Not really.

His nature, his character, it seemed to me, must have been formed long ago by unhappy forces over which neither he nor anybody else had control.

Loss

·────────────────────────────·

*F*OR A SHORT TIME *he had been my teacher at an art
school. Since I was the oldest in the class, already in my mid-twenties,
he had favored me with private conversations after he had given
corrections to the other students.*

We became friends.

*For a whole week after a heavy air raid on Berlin, he did not
show up for class. I worried. Finally I decided to look him up at his
private atelier, which wasn't far away from where I lived. Turning
into his street, I could see that a whole row of houses, his among
them, were empty shells. In a house across the street from where
he had lived, I inquired and after having talked to several people
who had no idea who had once lived opposite, I found a woman
who told me that most of the people in the destroyed houses had
perished, but Hans Speidel—yes, she knew him, the painter—had
survived. She even gave me the address of a friend's house where I
could find him.*

*I hardly recognized him when I entered his room. He seemed
to have aged years since I saw him a week ago. He was slumped in
a chair, his face buried in his hands, and his once-brown hair was
snowy white. Hearing my voice, he stretched out both his hands;
the right one was in a heavy bandage. His forehead, I could see
now, was creased from temple to temple with a wide, barely healed
wound.*

I pulled a chair close to his and sat down.

"I lost her," he said before I could ask any questions. "Lost, lost, lost," he repeated, his voice quivering.

I knew he was talking about his wife. He had told me about their harmonious and creative union: he, a painter, she, a sculptor.

"Do you want to know how it happened?" he asked, and, without waiting for my answer, he went on.

"It was a direct hit on our house. We hadn't heard anything, but suddenly a flood of water streamed into our air shelter. Within minutes it went up to our knees, to our hips, to our bellies. The house warden ordered us—about forty people—to follow him. He knew a way out of the cellar, he said. Through a long tunnel. In complete darkness, hindered by collapsed walls and slowed down by the force of the water, we struggled on. Inch by inch. To where? Nobody knew. The water was nearly up to our chests now.

"I held on to Ida's hand—it was warm and sticky with blood. She moaned. She stopped. She could not fight the water anymore. I could not make her move.

" 'Come,' I said.

" 'I can't,' she said.

"I pulled, wrested, throwing myself against the forceful masses of water. By now it was up to my chin. A tall man in front of me threw his arms around my neck and jerked me forward in an attempt to help me and . . . I lost Ida's hand.

"I tried to shake myself loose from my rescuer's grip. When I finally succeeded, I turned back to look for Ida. There was no trace of her in the black gurgling flood.

"She was gone . . . but I got out. How? I have no memory of it."
He paused.
I waited.
"And now?" he asked. "What now? I love her . . . I need her and I want her back . . . but I lost her . . . God have mercy on me."

Oskar
(Götterdämmerung)

WHEN I met him, his name was Haupt, Oskar Haupt: Haupt meaning *head*. But when he knew me better and trusted me, he told me his real name was Huth, Oskar Huth: Huth meaning *hat*.

He showed me his identification card and his army discharge paper made out for Oskar Haupt, and, with a smile, he whispered: "Homemade."

"Homemade?" I asked.

"Yes. I made them myself."

I looked at him in disbelief. He kept on smiling, nodding his head.

"How did you get the paper?"

"I made it."

"The paper has watermarks," I said.

"Of course. It has to."

"There are three different stamps of the Oberkommando der Wehrmacht on it," I said. "Where did you get them?"

"I got them from Oskar Huth," he said, grinning.

But that wasn't all. He pulled a whole sheet of butter ration coupons out of his pocket.

"Heavens!" I exclaimed. "These are good for pounds and pounds of butter." Our weekly ration of butter at that time was extremely small. "This will last you a year."

"No, it won't," Oskar said. "It has to help several people."

"What people?" I wanted to know.

"People who do not get food ration cards—officially. Because they don't exist—officially."

I was curious. I asked one question after another and slowly, bit by bit, I began to see the whole picture.

But let me begin at the beginning.

I had come to Berlin in September of 1938. The war had not broken out yet. I lived in furnished rooms, and moved rather frequently from one to another, always looking for a better one.

Though I did not have many friends during the first months in Berlin, I never felt lonely. There was so much to see, to hear, to experience. My afternoon secretarial job was dull, but the mornings in art school were not, and though I was much older than all the other students, I befriended some of them. On weekends, when I did not visit museums or go to concerts, I painted. Timidly and eclectically. But also happily.

Then came September 1, 1939. For those of us who had never trusted Hitler, who had seen him as a power-hungry lunatic, it was the confirmation of our fears when he viciously attacked Poland. We had witnessed already Hitler's ever-increasing criminal acts: the annexation of Austria and Czechoslovakia, the persecution of Jews, Gypsies, and homosexuals, the assault on art and literature. And yet most Germans still followed their Führer blindly. But now the great killing: open war!

Not too much changed in the life of the civilians in Berlin during the first war years. The blackout, of course, and the ration cards were a bother. Butter and milk had been rationed already, but now there was a long list of items which required coupons.

Also many dry goods were rationed, and people had to stand in long lines to get them.

In spite of the shortage of apartments, one day I was lucky. I found an especially nice half-furnished room in the Meinekestrasse. The Meinekestrasse was a linden-lined street just off the famous and glamorous Kurfürstendamm with its cafés and elegant shops, in the nice western part of Berlin.

Frau Lasker held the lease on the apartment. Only seldom did we meet each other in the kitchen. We exchanged friendly greetings and a few words, which never amounted to more than small talk. We both liked our privacy. Only much later, after the heavy bombardments altered everybody's life, did our relations change. Step by step we found out that we both were in the same camp: Hitler and his cohorts were our enemies. And then we trusted, liked, and helped each other whenever we could.

The new room I had moved into was much larger than any room I had lived in before. That meant I had space for an easel. I decided to get one.

I shopped around and found a nice, sturdy one, second-hand, and bought it. The clerk offered to carry it out to my car.

"I have no car," I told him.

"But, mein Fräulein! How will you, little lady, carry this large heavy easel?"

"I'm strong," I said and got a good hold on the easel. I could lift it from the floor, but I realized it was going to be very heavy and awkward to carry. I put it down and tried once more to get a better grip. Hearing laughter behind me, I turned and threw an angry look at the clerk. I was still wondering what to do when a slender young man approached me, a smile on his pale, thin face. A warm and understanding smile, and a nod.

"May I?" was all he said. Coming close to me, he picked up the easel and walked toward the door. I followed him.

"But—," I said.

"No but, mein Fräulein. Just tell me where the easel wants to go."

"Meinekestrasse," I replied. "It's rather far away and—"

"Only ten blocks," the stranger interjected and walked on briskly.

It was hard to keep up with him. I walked a few steps behind, marveling as the easel bobbed up and down with the rhythm of his gait. It extended far above the head of the carrier, a spindle-thin, almost delicate young man.

I caught up with him. "Let me help."

"No, no," he said.

"It's too heavy for you," I insisted.

"Think of the ants," he said. "They often lug pieces two or three times their size."

"But you aren't an ant."

"Wish I were," he said, then grinned and quickened his pace to be ahead of me again.

"Stop," I said when we reached Meinekestrasse 21. "Here is where I live."

I thanked him warmly. I wanted to say good-bye, but he asked me to open the door. He carried the easel through the courtyard and ordered me to open the next door, the door to my apartment. Only when we were in my room did he put the easel down.

He said it had been a pleasure to carry my easel, a "noble piece of furniture," he called it, and then he said, "Good-bye, see you again," and left.

I ran after him. "My name is Ilse. Ilse Vogel. Come to see me again!"

Did he hear me? I didn't know. He turned his head for a moment, waved, and hurried away.

Weeks went by. Months. He never came. I went to the store where I had bought the easel, hoping to find out who he was. Nobody knew him, though they said he came every once in a while to buy canvas, paints, and drawing papers.

I could not forget him. The easel was a steady reminder. I sometimes put my beret (he had worn a navy blue one) on the easel and talked to it as if it were him. Years passed, and then I met him again.

Christa had asked me to visit her. Arriving at her apartment, I found her in animated conversation with my easel carrier.

"Death to him!" I heard him hiss in a low, furious voice.

Seeing me, he jumped up, greeted me joyously, and asked, "How is our easel? Did it serve you well?"

Christa was startled. "You know each other?"

"I know him," I said laughing, "though I don't really know who he is."

Now he told Christa how we had met. Christa was amused and, in a mock-serious and official voice, she said, "May I introduce you to Oskar Haupt. A veteran of the anti-Hitler army."

"Splendid," I said.

"Splendid," Christa echoed. "Splendid also how he manages to stay out of a gray, black, or brown uniform. Isn't it?"

I nodded and turned to Oskar. "How do you manage that?"

"Well," he said, frowning but grinning at the same time. "Well, . . . I don't want to seem arrogant or boastful—but one has to have certain talents."

"And where is the battleground of your army?" I asked.

Shrugging, he answered, "In my basement, more or less."

But before I could ask more questions, Oskar happily declared, "The Russians are pushing into Romania. Maybe they will be in Berlin before Christmas, and the war will be over."

"Heavens!" Christa exclaimed. "If that's the case, I have to get out of Berlin. The day *and* night bombardments we have now are already more than I can take. But the Russians . . ."

I was surprised that Christa seemed to have succumbed to the Goebbels propaganda about the "beastly" Russians and wanted to say so.

But Oskar changed the subject by pulling a small wooden flute, a recorder, out of the inner pocket of his jacket. "How about a little Mozart?" he asked and, without waiting for our approval, he soothed us with a heavenly melody.

When Oskar and I left an hour later, he insisted on walking me home. His first words were, "Isn't she lovely?"

"Yes, she is," I said without hesitating.

For a long time we walked in silence. The streets were empty. The blackout was complete. Only the nearly full moon did not cooperate. The skeletons of the burned-out houses stood ghostly black against the bright, moonlit sky.

"Horrible, but kind of pretty," Oskar said after a while. "Though the ruins of the fifteenth-century castles along the Rhine and Mosel are prettier."

"I've never seen them," I said. "Do you think Berlin will remain in ruins for centuries to come?"

"No," Oskar said determinedly. "Germans are insurmountable. For better or worse, I don't know. Germans, whatever is left of them, will immediately and antlike rebuild their towns and cities the moment the war is over."

We turned a corner and suddenly were face to face with the

moon. We both stopped walking and stared at her. Then Oskar took out his little wooden flute again and played a folk song, a tender tune. I sang the words as Oskar played.

"Guter Mond, du gehst so stille durch die Abendwolken hin."

(Good moon, you move so quietly through the evening clouds.)

I was moved, and Oskar seemed so, too. The song finished, we walked on again.

"Do you know Christa well?" Oskar asked.

"I don't know," I replied. "She is a very complex person."

"Yes," Oskar agreed, "and hard to figure out. Do you like her?"

"Very much. And you?"

A long pause.

"I *love* her," Oskar said in a low voice. Then he continued, "We met years ago in the life class at the Art Academy. To tell the truth, I seldom drew the model. I always drew her. She was so beautiful."

"Was?" I interjected. "She still is!"

"Of course she is. But a certain kind of mellowness her features had shortly after she arrived in the big city has now been replaced by a sophisticated, knowing kind of expression. I guess you know she came from Pomerania—grew up in a parsonage there."

"Yes, I do."

"I've wooed her for many years," Oskar went on, "but have never gotten the slightest encouragement. The opposite: she remains cool and aloof."

"But you seem to share many interests, don't you?"

"Politics, art, and music maybe. That's all."

Oskar stopped walking.

"Why am I telling you all this?" he said with a forced little laugh. And answered himself immediately: "It must be the moon that makes me so sentimental. And so talkative . . . to a mere stranger."

"I don't feel as if we were strangers," I comforted. "After all, we've known each other for years."

Oskar reached for my hand, kissed it hastily, and said, "Thank you. May I call you Ilse?"

"Of course, Oskar," I replied.

"Are we friends now?" he asked.

"Of course, Oskar," I said.

That was how our long and close friendship began.

From then on Oskar dropped in frequently and at the most unexpected times: sometimes early in the morning, sometimes late at night. Sometimes he asked whether he could stay over. He didn't have his own place yet, he explained. A few cushions on the floor let him sleep deep and well. I didn't mind. I liked it. Before he went to sleep, he usually played a little Mozart or Bach on his recorder. That helped me, who suffered from insomnia, to fall asleep.

And when I woke up in the morning, he was always gone.

I liked that, too. Mornings were always hard for me. I was withdrawn, not yet ready to talk to anybody. And no coffee was available anymore to help overcome the morning blues.

For several weeks I did not see Oskar. Then, one Sunday morning, he arrived, radiant. He now had a place to stay. Friends had left the city because they could no longer endure the increasing bombardments, and Oskar was allowed to stay at their apartment in Wilmersdorf, on the outskirts of Berlin.

"Come with me," he said. "I want you to see one of my most precious possessions. It's now stored there."

"What is it?" I asked.

"You'll see" was all he said.

When we were outside, Oskar said, "Since it's a nice, sunny day, let's walk."

Had I known how far from my place his was, I might have said no. But I didn't. So we walked to the end of the Kurfürstendamm, passing rows and rows of roofless houses. People, though in danger from the dangling girders and beams, searched through the ashes hoping to find remnants of their belongings.

"Remember Goering's promise at the beginning of the war?" Oskar asked. "He boasted, 'You can call me *Meier* if ever a bomb falls on Germany.'"

We laughed—though it was not a laughing matter at all.

"Look!" Suddenly Oskar stopped in front of a house. "Look," he said again, "just like a dollhouse."

And, indeed, only the facade had been blown away, leaving all the rooms in full view. They seemed in perfect order: the furniture in place, even paintings and mirrors on the walls. Oskar got very excited.

"Look," he said once more, "a grand piano on the third floor! It's a Bechstein, I bet."

There was no way to hold him back. I watched as he dashed up the stairs. When he reached the third floor, he immediately sat down at the piano. The waltz from Strauss's *Rosenkavalier* floated down to me. I stood entranced. There was, for minutes, no room for other thoughts in my head. I was hardly aware of the bizarre surroundings. Oskar played on and on for quite some time. When the music ended, I felt as if I were coming out of a dream.

I didn't see Oskar descend. He had to tug on my hand to start me walking.

Not many people were in the streets on this cold Sunday

morning. The few we met were lugging huge bundles or pulling small makeshift carts loaded with pots and pans, with blankets and pillows, even mattresses, things they had salvaged from their destroyed dwellings. In one of the carts, pulled by two teenage boys, huddled an ancient woman on top of a mountain of pillows. A tiny baby lay crying in her lap.

When Oskar saw that I was close to crying too, he said, "Think of them as super-Nazis. That's the only way one can bear a sight like this."

It was a thought, though it didn't help me much. Silently we walked on. Turning into a side street, we saw people lined up in front of one house still standing in a row of demolished ones. I was surprised. Queues like this usually formed in front of grocery stores. But today, Sunday, they were all closed.

"It's a cinema," Oskar said. "A circus film is playing."

"Amazing," I said, "how many people flock to the movie houses. To escape to a fantasy world, I guess. And . . . I don't blame them."

A little later we passed a bar. Through the half-open door, we saw soldiers and women devotedly listening to someone singing "Lili Marlene."

"The bars are full, the churches are empty," Oskar commented. We found fewer houses destroyed as we moved further away from the center of the city. And when we turned into Oskar's street, there were rows of medium-sized houses, small lawns separating them from the street, that had not yet suffered any damage. In one of them Oskar lived. His three-room apartment was pleasant; the rooms were not very large and furnished in the typical way of the German middle class. But there was a surprise in one of the rooms: a beautiful clavichord.

Oskar moved his hand caressingly over its top, which was inlaid with mother-of-pearl and ivory.

"Homemade too," he said.

"You mean you made it yourself?" I asked.

Oskar nodded. He sat down and began to play, but he was instantly interrupted by the howling of the air-raid sirens.

"Come," he said, "we must go to the basement shelter."

"You go if you want to," I said defiantly. "You know that I never go to a shelter."

"But here you must, Ilse, please. Because *I* must be seen by the inhabitants of the house. I have to behave in as normal a way as possible. I can't afford to draw attention to myself."

I still hesitated.

"Besides," Oskar said, "you will see my workroom. My laboratory, so to say—also my battleground."

That aroused my curiosity, and I followed him.

Oskar greeted the crowd in the basement with a cheerful Heil Hitler, introduced me as his colleague Erika, and said these nuisance air raids always gave him an opportunity to catch up on the work he had to do on his printing press. Saying that, he unlocked the padlock on a slatted door leading to a space partitioned off from the main basement.

"Today," he said, his voice raised so that everybody could hear him, "I must print a pamphlet about the findings of my boss, the veterinarian Dr. Peppers. It concerns the so-called holiday disease of horses."

We entered the stall. I didn't know what to make of the heavy piece of equipment standing in the center of the cramped little room. Soon, however, Oskar inserted a sheet of blank paper into it, pulled a switch, which made the whole thing rattle loudly, and moments later he pulled out a printed sheet of butter coupons.

He put a finger to his lips to silence me, but that wasn't necessary. I was speechless.

He continued until he had about a dozen sheets printed. Then he stopped. Quickly he picked up a different sheet of paper, readied for his purpose, and stepped outside the stall to join the crowd.

They were well entertained when Oskar read to them what they believed he had just printed. Namely that workhorses, used to heavy work, get sick when they have not worked for some time. This disease, lumbago, also called holiday sickness, causes a chemical change in the muscle structure and leads to lameness.

Oscar could not finish reading the whole report because the all clear sounded and everybody left. Oskar led me back to the printing stall. It was then and there he told me about his clandestine existence: How Oskar Huth had become Oskar Haupt. How he, knowing the process of papermaking (starting with linen rags or wood pulp), could make paper or, in many cases, treat certain papers to resemble those used for identification cards, official certificates, and ration coupons.

I was impressed.

I interrupted Oskar to tell him how I admired his unique ability and also his desire to help so many endangered people.

"Hold it, hold it," Oskar said. "I'm not quite so saintly as you might think. If you want to know the truth, it all started with sheer selfishness on my part. It began when I received my draft notice. From that moment on, there was only one thought in my mind: how to save my own skin. I didn't want to die for a lunatic like Hitler! I didn't want to fight for the victory of the Thousand Year Reich. You see, Ilse, that's how it began. Awful, isn't it?"

"No," I said, "it isn't. And you are helping many people now!"

"Of course," Oskar said. "There are others who also deserve to survive."

Then Oskar went on to tell me more: How, after a long search, he had found a small printing press in an out-of-business printing plant. How he also found bundles of old paper stock, paper he knew he could "cure" to make it look and feel like the paper used by the military and the party organizations. He showed me rubber stamps he had made with the insignia of the Oberkommando der Wehrmacht and stamps of the Labor Department and an array of stamps for different police precincts all over Germany.

"These have helped not only me, but also a lot of other people—Jews, deserters, anti-Nazis—helped them to escape and survive," Oskar said.

"And you do all this, the printing I mean, so openly?" I asked. "Down here, in the presence of so many people?"

"Of course. The openness eliminates all suspicion. Look, the press is installed in such a way that the people from one side can see that I am printing. But what lies behind the head of the press, where the printed paper comes out, they cannot see. That I'm doing it in their presence, even during the bombardments, makes it seem utterly legal."

I was impressed, but also worried. Couldn't he be found out?

Oskar, who was watching me intently, stopped speaking. He smiled and pulled two objects out of his pocket: his wooden flute and a small pistol. "These two keep my mind at peace," he said. He twirled the pistol in his hand and added, "Only to be used in case of utmost emergency. You know, I'm really not very keen on killing people."

The hilarity with which he said this put me off.

Oskar, realizing this, looked at me and asked, "Maybe you don't like the new Oskar? The Oskar you just met?"

"I like him fine," I replied.

Oskar locked his stall, and we went upstairs. He sat down at his clavichord again.

"May I?" he asked and instantly began to play. A complete change came over him: his head, slightly bent, swayed with the rhythm of the music. His pale, thin fingers glided, it seemed lovingly, over the keyboard, and serenity replaced a certain anguished expression in his face. I, sitting on a sofa, closed my eyes and let the music take hold of me. Oskar played for an hour.

He must have thought I had fallen asleep.

"Sorry, I bored you," I heard him say.

I shook my head. Oskar got up and sat down beside me.

"Ilse," he said, "now I have to do something you might not like at all."

The tone of his voice disconcerted me.

"Why so serious?" I asked.

"Because this is serious," he replied while pulling out a second pistol, a very small one, from under a pillow.

"Take it," he said.

I pushed his hand away. "Never," I said sternly. "Never."

"Listen," he said and then explained to me that we, who had not joined the war effort, might be seen as the "enemy within." The reason the war was lost. It had happened after the first World War; it could easily happen again and result in life-threatening attacks on people like us.

"Be sensible, Ilse," he urged. "Now watch."

He showed me how the revolver functioned.

"I hope it isn't loaded," I admonished.

"Of course not," Oskar assured me.

He had just said this when the gun went off. A bullet went

between Oskar's head and mine and ricocheted from the wall behind us.

The blast deafened me. I was paralyzed, unable to say a word.

But Oskar, to my great consternation, burst out laughing. So hysterical was his non-ending laughter that it frightened me.

I had sometimes, during my friendship with Oskar, been surprised by his rapid mood changes. His caustic humor and bitter, serious talk could suddenly change to sheer daftness, to laughter and jokes. Often this seemed a welcome release and made me laugh, too. I knew Oskar was a man walking a tightrope, a pit filled with lions below him. Sometimes he needed to discharge accumulated tension, and one could not measure or judge him by ordinary rules.

But right now I could not join in his laughter. I remained seated, covering my ringing ears with my hands.

Oskar's laughter did not diminish; it suddenly stopped. He put the pistol back under the pillow and pulled my hands from my ears.

"Oh, Ilse," he pleaded, "my dear Ilse." And, patting me on my shoulder, he asked. "Do you know what has been proven to us right now? That we—not the Nazis—are indestructible."

It seemed a strange and farfetched conclusion to me.

But I nodded when he asked, "You will forgive me, won't you?"

I still felt giddy when Oskar brought me to the nearby subway station. He told me that this line, which had been heavily bombed only three days before, was already working again.

There were many surprises like this all over the city. All means of transportation were always promptly restored. The working population, many of them still holding war-essential jobs, had to be brought to their workplaces. Also the telephone cables, frequently damaged, were usually quickly repaired. And entertainment, concerts, cinema, even variety shows were supported by the government in order to pacify the people and create the illusion of normal life.

As time passed, the situation got rapidly worse.

The air attacks increased from day to day. As a result, certain aspects of life became more difficult, others easier. Easier because the chaos in the city after the heavy bombardments was often beyond the control of the government and the bureaucracy.

Oskar observed all this with a fiendish kind of enthusiasm and drew his own conclusions. He did not trust Germans anymore. He thought that all of Germany should, after the end of the war, come under foreign, maybe American jurisdiction.

I, politically naive, had only one wish: to bring the Thousand Year Reich to an end as quickly as possible and to get rid of all and everybody who had been part of it. Having so many like-minded, Hitler-hating friends, I hoped there would be enough of us left to build a new democratic Germany.

Oskar came frequently, though irregularly, to see me. Sometimes he showed up twice a day, sometimes not for a whole week.

My friends, who had met him (as Oskar Haupt, of course), liked him, too. And our gatherings were not always gloomy in "Ilse's Park," as my friends called my room, with its many trees and bushes. Oskar, having a great sense of humor (dark, biting humor at times), would clown a little, would do little magic tricks or play his wooden flute. It was astonishing how he could hush a noisy room. And, strangely enough, he did it by whispering. Never did he raise his voice. Even when his hatred for Hitler made him use the most violent language, his voice remained low, even tender.

Everybody wanted to hear what he, in his quiet and unique way, had to say. Oskar's way of speaking was flowery. He often digressed, but without ever losing the main thread. He talked a lot about politics, but preferred to talk about music and musical instruments. He could describe the inner mechanics of a large organ or a piano in such vivid and poetic terms that this in itself seemed like music. Everyone would sit leaning forward, spellbound.

Sometimes I helped Oskar to cure his paper. It was a complicated process that I did not fully understand. For me, Oskar became a sorcerer when he, with nimble fingers, opened small bottles and let drop after drop of a strong-smelling liquid fall into a water-filled basin. Then he added carefully measured amounts of several powders to the solution and tested it with litmus paper before declaring it perfect.

I also helped with the tedious work of exchanging butter coupons for butter. Oskar had many friends living underground whom he supplied. Of course, nobody could go to one store and buy a pound or even a half a pound of butter at once. In order not to arouse suspicion we had to buy the allotment for one week only: a few grams.

It took some footwork to get several pounds together. I could not go to the stores in my neighborhood too frequently, which meant going to stores often quite far away.

Butter coupons brought high prices on the black market. And in order to support himself and his friends living illegally, Oskar sometimes sold coupons to people who took him for an ordinary black marketeer. My landlady, for instance, was delighted to purchase coupons for a price lower than the usual price on the black market.

In the long hours I spent with Oskar, I gradually learned more about his past. It had startled me, when I first met him, how extremely white his complexion was. Soon it became obvious that he avoided sunshine as if it were poisonous. He always chose the shady side of the street, even though it meant going out of his way. I, like many Germans and people living in the northern regions of Europe, was a sun lover. I was curious, and one day I asked him about this.

As a very young man, he explained, he had suffered too much from tropical sun and heat.

"Tropical heat?" I asked. "Where?"

And then he told me one of the many grim stories his youth seemed to be full of. He was fifteen years old when his father contracted him to the merchant marine. His job was as a stoker on a freighter that sailed between Hamburg and India. Every day he endured twelve hours of shoveling coal into the furnace, and a beastly captain who seldom let the working crew step on deck. Then came a week-long sojourn in a hell-hot, humid Indian harbor, loading the freighter for the return trip.

"Night," said Oskar and made it sound like the beginning of a poem. "Dark, cool nights. That's what I like best."

His next report, gruesome too, had to do with cold and should have balanced out his feelings against the sun and heat. But it didn't.

Oskar's father was an organ builder and tuner. His profession took him from village to village, from church to church. It just so happened that most churches wanted their organs tuned or repaired during the winter, shortly after Christmas. The unheated churches were bitterly cold. Icy. Oskar, eight years old and frail, had to carry heavy organ pipes, often eight to ten feet long. He had to hold them completely steady while his father, after having cleaned them, reset them. Oskar's fingers felt as if they were frozen stiff in spite of gloves. His whole body trembled with cold, including his fingers. A sharp rap on his wrist or his head was his punishment when he moved. Hours and hours passed, interrupted only by a quick sip of malt coffee from a thermos bottle and a hasty bite from a meager, tasteless sandwich.

"How could you have stood it?" I asked.

"Aaah," Oskar said, and a glow lit up his face. "When Father was done, he *played* the organ. And already at that age music was heaven for me. Those five or ten minutes of Bach literally warmed me and erased the hours of suffering."

"I'm surprised you didn't choose to become a musician. Why didn't you?"

"Aaah," Oskar said again. "Because there were museums. So many fine museums in Berlin. And they did something to me."

"What did they do?" I asked.

"One Sunday morning a visiting uncle dragged me, much against my wishes, to the Kaiser Friedrich Museum. And it only took a short time before I was overwhelmed, really overwhelmed, by what I saw. There were the landscapes I would have liked to live in. There were the women and children I would have loved to be with. In the beginning it was as superficial a reaction as this to the masterpieces I was looking at. But it brought me back to the museum week after week after week. You can understand that, Ilse, can't you?"

I nodded eagerly, and Oskar went on to tell me that he soon had the desire to paint. He started by drawing. He would keep a certain painting he had seen in the museum close to his mind's eye and, arriving at home, sit down and draw what he remembered. He improved the drawings after each museum visit. He did this for many weeks.

One day, he told me, he had enough courage to take the drawing with him to the museum for comparison, and he was surprised how much it resembled the original.

The next step was color. Paints were expensive, but somehow he managed to buy some. The paintings that now took shape on inexpensive cotton canvas brought him hours of great pleasure. He continued to draw and paint at home, until one day he dared to take his paint box and a small easel to the museum. He set it up in front of a moonlit Caspar David Friedrich landscape and began to paint. Happily.

A heavy hand on his shoulder came as a shock. "What are you doing, young man?" the museum guard asked. "Do you have a permit for copying?"

Before Oskar could answer, the guard shook his head.

"Of course not. You are much too young to have one." And he ordered Oskar to leave.

Crestfallen and discouraged, Oskar went home. But he did not give up painting. From postcard reproductions he painted one painting after another. His desire to copy the museum's paintings, however, became so strong that one day he composed a letter to the director of the museum.

Dear Sir,
    Please have the kindness to allow me to show you some of my work. I am a painter, but, as the rules of your museum say, too young to be allowed to copy paintings, paintings to which I am drawn with all my heart. Humbly waiting

for your kind response, I remain devotedly your Oskar Huth.

He added one of his drawings to the letter.

A week later, with as many paintings as he could carry, Oskar was on his way to the museum. He described the half hour in the impressive reception room of the museum director, with his heart beating fast, his cheeks flushing to a crimson red, and the anxiety that made him lose his tongue and made his hands tremble. All this made me tremble, too.

But in the end, Oskar walked out with a copying permit in his hand and the assurance that he was the only youngster ever to receive such a permit. Oskar was proud.

Long, happy hours in the museum followed and, best of all, Oskar was now able to sell some of his copies. Proud of her son's achievement, his mother showed Oskar's paintings to her friends and neighbors. Remembering a certain sale, Oskar burst out laughing.

"I had copied a beautiful large Courbet," he told me. "The inside of a forest. I asked a rather steep price for it because my supply of canvas and paints had gotten very low. The baker's wife, to whom my mother showed it, was impressed. The price was high, she said, but she would pay it if I would put a deer in the forest. A stag. And preferably the Saint Hubertus stag, a mythical animal whose antlers ended in burning candles."

"And did you?" I asked.

"Of course. I needed the money."

After Oskar had hummed a tune to himself, he continued. "Well, this was not quite as shameful as what I had to do later— in a situation where I was desperate for money."

"Do you want to tell me?" I asked.

"Why not," Oskar said, smiling. And without telling me why or how he happened to be in Hamburg penniless, he described in detail the complicated process of casting coins, by which he counterfeited five-pfennig pieces.

"All this effort for a few pennies?" I asked.

"Yes, just enough to buy bread. Only bread."

"Maybe," I said, "you felt the smaller the coin, the smaller the crime."

"Perhaps. Something like that, perhaps. I don't really know."

Where was the yardstick, I wondered, with which to measure crime when nowadays crimes were made into laws?

"I didn't feel especially guilty then," Oskar continued. "I felt I wasn't harming anyone in particular, and I did it only until I had enough money for a railway ticket back to Berlin."

I asked more questions, but Oskar didn't answer. Instead he reached for his recorder. "I feel like music now," he said and began to play.

I, however, was left in a strange state of unbalance and confusion. Good, bad, right or wrong—who was the judge? Was one's own conscience the only guide?

The Mozart sonata washed away some of these bothersome thoughts. It soothed and comforted.

The music finished, Oskar left abruptly, and I didn't see him for several days.

A dark Christmas came—three candles were all I could get hold of—and brought 1944 to an end. Daily, hundreds of Berliners left the city.

One day Oskar came and reported, crestfallen, that Christa had left, too. Where had she gone, he did not know. He was unusually quiet and withdrawn. He didn't talk. He didn't even play his wooden flute. Slumped in a chair, he just brooded.

"I should have told her," he suddenly said. "I should have!"

"What?" I asked. "And to whom?"

"Oh, to Christa. I should have told her I love her."

"You never did?"

"No, I didn't. And now it's too late. I may never see her again."

"You know, Oskar, one should never say never." That was all I could think of to comfort him.

"Are you sure, Ilse, you don't want to get out of Berlin?" Oskar asked one day when we walked past burned-out houses, ashes still glowing from fires started days before. Our eyes were smarting, our throats burning.

"Get out?" I asked, surprised.

But this question, coming from Oskar, made me for the first time ask myself why it had never occurred to me during all these harrowing years.

"Get out?" I repeated. "Where to? And why now . . . when the end is so near?"

"The end might not be so cozy," Oskar said.

"I guess not," I said, "but I feel I belong here. And furthermore, I want to be present at the new beginning. I see it as a reward for all I have endured in this city."

"I'm afraid you are a bit callow, Ilse. But . . . I understand."

I was glad *he* understood because, right now, I couldn't understand myself. What made me so fearless? My friends often called me courageous, but it was not courage at all that caused me to do all kinds of reckless things. Who in his right mind would, instead of going to an air-raid shelter, stand on rooftops during bombardments, marveling at what was going on in the night sky? It really was an extraordinary sight: blue, red, and yellow "Christmas trees," as the Germans called these cone-shaped flares, floating slowly to the ground. They were signals, set by Allied spotting planes, to mark targets for the bombers that followed. Gigantic searchlight beams crisscrossed each other forming enormous stars in the black sky. Anti-aircraft fire drew sparkling arcs all over the city. More impressive fireworks I had never seen.

No, this had nothing to do with courage. It was a mixture of curiosity and fatalism that held me in Berlin. And also brought me to rooftops.

The visual pleasure of this spectacle was indeed great. It was, however, heavily paid for by the feeling of guilt from taking pleasure in so devastating and often fatal an event. Had I become a monster too, I sometimes wondered. There had even been moments when, during the air attacks, I had wished them to be more devastating. An adage, better an end with horror than a horror without end, had crossed my mind and led me to cruel and inhuman conclusions.

I wanted to explain this to Oskar, but before I could say a word, he said, "I know. I know we are both fatalists."

These words seemed like a seal on our friendship. And instinctively I knew at that moment that we would, together, live through or die in the final battle, the battle of Berlin.

It came sooner than we had expected. We knew that since the beginning of March the west as well as the east front was approximately one hundred miles from Berlin. We saw the results of the insane order, given by the Berlin officials, to defend the city. Ditches were dug at main arteries. Streets were blocked by overturned trucks and streetcars filled with stones.

Young boys, children really, stuck in uniforms much too large for them, patrolled the streets carrying bazookas. Some looked defiant and visibly proud to be soldiers of sorts, others timid and obviously dreadfully scared.

We also saw columns of refugees from the eastern part of Germany dragging through the streets. Some of them towed goats, sheep, and even cows on leashes, shoeless children at their sides. Where were they going? The city had no means to give them shelter.

We saw all these miseries and many, many more. And as hard as life was for us, it seemed luxurious to me, compared to the sufferings of these silent columns. Apathy and exhaustion must have taken their voices away.

One day—it was the middle of April now—Oskar arrived with a smile on his face and two tickets in his hand.

"The philharmonic!" he announced, jubilant. "We are going to a concert in Beethoven Hall."

I couldn't believe it. "A concert?" I asked.

"Yes, the philharmonic is still performing. And I was lucky to barter two tickets."

On a cloud of joy, we walked to Beethoven Hall in Berlin Center. I tried to preserve my happiness in looking forward to the concert by keeping my eyes on the ground, so I would not see the burned-out houses to the right and the left of us. And . . . I was rewarded: in the cracked concrete of the sidewalk glowed a bright yellow star. A dandelion! Surrounded by a clump of green. I showed it to Oskar. He smiled, muttered something like "Oh, yes, nature" and "survival," but urged me on so that we would not miss the beginning of the concert.

For a long time, all kinds of entertainment—theater, concerts, films—had begun in the afternoon to give people enough time to be home before nine o'clock, when the air raids usually started.

At four o'clock Beethoven Hall was filled to capacity. The quiet was churchlike. Balm to the soul. The big, beautiful hall was still intact and allowed a prewar feeling to arise in me.

The first part of the concert was devoted to Beethoven, the second to Wagner.

"Very appropriate," Oskar said when he saw *Die Götterdämmerung*. Wagner's tragic music of the death of the gods was the last piece on the program.

"I wish there was more Beethoven," I whispered in Oskar's ear.

One of Beethoven's sonatas I knew very well, and its melody transported me back to my childhood—to my bed, upstairs, in the big country house of my parents. Downstairs my mother played the Beethoven sonata on the piano, and the music floated up to my room, arousing an indescribable feeling of well-being inside me. For a moment, I could refeel it now. I waited for a certain passage I used to like especially. The music was slowly building up to it, and when it came, I was surprised that there were notes I did not remember at all: short, dull thuds, very unlike any sound a piano could produce.

Oskar and I looked at each other questioningly.

"Something wrong with the piano," Oskar whispered.

When the concert was over, we left Beethoven Hall reluctantly, still under the spell of the music. It was a sobering shock to step out into the smoky, acrid air.

A few steps, and a sound unfamiliar to our ears made us stop and listen: a boom, followed after a few seconds by boom after boom after boom. Distant and dull. A bit like thunder from a storm far away, and yet different.

It made the air tremble.

Even before I could ask what it was, Oskar said, "Artillery. The Russians."

At that moment, it became clear to us that this must have been the sound that had startled us during the Beethoven sonata.

The people in the street were all in a great hurry. Yet frequently they stopped, held their breath, and listened. They exchanged bewildered glances and, shaking their heads, continued walking.

We hurried back to my place and switched on the radio. The Wehrmacht communiqué was short, not giving much information. The weather report, however, coming from Potsdam, was long and detailed. The forecast promised the following day would be unusually mild, with temperatures in the sixties and the possibility of a thunderstorm.

"We are close now," Oskar said. "Close to the end."

He wanted to go home once more to fetch some important things.

"My toothbrush, for instance," he said, grinning and baring his brownish teeth, slightly deformed from malnutrition and scurvy in his youth. "These beauties have to be taken care of, come what may," he added. "I'll also bring the pistol for you."

"I don't want it. I told you so. I have my cyanide."

"With cyanide you cannot kill anybody who wants to kill you."

"Who would want to kill me?" I asked.

"Well, I told you there might be people, remember?"

"Oh, yes, the stab-in-the-back legend. Forget about it. I am much more worried about you, in your civilian clothes, still walking the streets."

And I reminded him of two corpses we had seen. Two young men in civilian clothing, dangling from lampposts: traitor signs pinned to their trousers.

But I could not dissuade Oskar. He left.

Anxiously I waited for his return. There was a knock at the door, and I hurried to open it.

But it was only Bruno, a friend of my landlady. He had a large, fully stuffed sack over his shoulder.

"Hi, darling," he said.

I didn't like being called darling by Bruno.

"We will set up camp here," he continued, "and prudently share what we have."

He pinched my cheek, grinned, and put down the heavy sack. Proudly he showed me cans and cans of food.

"All hoarded for this occasion," he said.

"What occasion?" I asked.

"Don't tell me you don't know these are the very last days of the Thousand Year Reich? And when it's over," he giggled, "I mean when peace breaks out, honey and manna will not flow immediately. We will not even have the skimpy food rations we are used to. Then, my darling, we will have to live on these goodies." He made the cans rattle in the sack.

Years ago Bruno, a huge and jolly man, had worked for a newspaper. His sharp, witty, and aggressive tongue had made him a successful reporter on one of Berlin's large tabloids. When his editor found out that Bruno was not an ardent Hitler supporter, he fired him. But Bruno, audacious and speaking English well, got a small job as a translator at the office that intercepted letters coming from abroad. His main duty was to black out lines or paragraphs, sometimes whole letters, containing information or opinions that should not reach the recipient.

"Someday I'll get caught and fired again, or even worse," he had confided in me, "because I don't strictly follow regulations. I don't black out as much as I should. I'm only too happy if some Germans, who are forbidden to listen to broadcasts from abroad, do hear our enemies'—God bless them!—opinions."

I did not really like Bruno, though I knew that inside this rough-looking man beat a friendly heart. And I thought maybe he was a good addition to our little household preparing for the big assault.

"My sister will be here soon, too," he said walking toward Frau Lasker, who had stepped into the corridor.

Oskar returned in the evening just as the air-raid sirens sounded.

"I had a close call," he explained. "but I don't want to talk about it." He seemed more shaken than I had ever seen him.

He, too, had a bag filled with cans of all kinds. And, trying to make me smile, he produced his toothbrush.

"Now I'm here to stay to the end with you," he said. "That is, if you let me."

Oskar could not shake his gloom. At first I accepted it. I didn't want to pry. But much later, when it was pitch-dark in the room, and we wanted to go to sleep, I heard him tossing on his cushions in the corner.

"Oskar," I said, "what is it? Please tell me, please."

It took a while before he began to talk.

"On my way back, I stopped at the Alberts'. As you know, they've been hiding the son of their Jewish friends who were deported two years ago. Hans, nine years old, lived in a small space in their basement, which they had made as comfortable as possible.

"Well, Hans got sick. Very sick—shaking with fever. And they didn't know a trustworthy physician. They did everything they could. They loved Hans as if he were their own child. But . . . Hans died. And then . . . well . . . what do you do with the corpse of a boy who officially does not exist?"

Oh, my God, I thought.

Oskar's voice was choked when he continued. "They wrapped him in a blanket and, at night, carried him far away and set him up in the doorway of a partly demolished building."

A long silence. Then . . . Oskar's flute.

It was nearly morning when we became aware of a great commotion in the hall outside the apartment. Oskar went to check.

"That's perfect," he declared when he came back. "Four German soldiers are laying down an eight-foot-long gasoline tank directly in front of our door. One small bit of shrapnel hits it, and the whole house will go up in flames."

"It won't," I said quickly and thoughtlessly. I just didn't want to give in to the increasing gloom and despair.

Oskar looked at me pityingly. Then, as if nothing was at stake, he pulled out his wooden flute and played. He played until a smile returned to my face.

The muffled thunder of the advancing Russian army came closer and got louder every day. What was really happening nobody knew. No official announcements had been made. Rumors and speculations flourished: The Russians were already in the eastern suburbs. They were raping and plundering and setting houses, not yet destroyed, on fire. And yet, some people still went on with their business, trying to lead a normal life.

"You can't go out into the street anymore," I told Oskar. "At least not as a man."

"What do you mean?" he asked.

"Well, I've given it quite some thought, Oksar, and you must agree to my plan."

"Which is?" he asked.

"Which is to dress you as a girl."

To my surprise, Oskar did not refuse. He instantly changed his whole demeanor. He tilted his head, folded his hands, little fingers raised, in front of his chest and, with swaying hips and tiny steps, he crossed the room and stopped before a mirror. He pulled his hair from behind his ears and pushed it forward toward his cheeks.

I grabbed one of my hats and put it on his head.

"Oh, thank you," he said, raising the pitch of his voice.

"It will work, it will work!" I exclaimed excitedly. "But now let's be serious."

I spread a few of my dresses out on the couch.

"Which one would you feel best in?" I asked. "They'll fit you well."

Fortunately we were the same height, Oskar just a bit thinner than I. He picked a flowered wool dress.

"No," I said, "this won't do. We will have a problem with your feet. Your shoes, I mean. Here, this very sporty outfit, a turtleneck pullover with the heavy corduroy skirt, will be much better. With this you can wear thick woolen stockings and heavy sport shoes—your own, as a matter of fact. Go to the bathroom, have a very close shave, and get dressed."

A short while later, Oskar-girl entered my room. The effect was startling. But I picked another hat, a tighter-fitting cap for him, which allowed only a wisp of hair to show, put some lipstick on his lips and a touch of rouge on his pale cheeks.

Together we stepped in front of the mirror again and laughed. Laughed triumphantly and heartily. The laughter did us good.

"Let's see whether it works," I said and made Oskar leave the apartment and ring Frau Lasker's doorbell.

She came, opened the door, and answered the stranger's question, whether Frau Vogel was home, with, "Yes, I think so. Come in." Then she knocked at my door and announced that a girl was coming to see me.

We carried on this charade for several more minutes before Oskar pulled off his cap in front of Frau Lasker's eyes and spoke in his baritone voice.

She opened her mouth wide, stared, and gasped, and finally clapped her hands in approval.

Now Oskar had enough courage to go out. Together we went to store after store and exchanged his coupons for bread and butter. I carefully watched the people who came in contact with Oskar-girl. Nobody paid any attention to him. But I also watched Oskar and could see that he was not comfortable. I was afraid that he, searching the eyes of people surrounding him, could draw attention to himself.

After all the coupons were spent, I went home. But Oskar

wanted to deliver the food immediately to his friends. They were scattered all over the city. Some lived on the outskirts in tiny huts people liked to set up on a small piece of land, called *Schrebergarten*, community gardens, to satisfy a city dweller's yearning for a bit of soil in which to grow a flower or a tomato.

Late in the afternoon, Oskar returned.

"I'm sure this was the last time I'll be able to get anything to those poor devils," he said.

Then he told me how afraid at first—and amused later—his friends were when an unknown "girl" approached their hiding places.

"And their mood?" I asked.

"A mixture of joy and fear now that they can *hear* the advancing front. And, like all of us, they don't know: Will this mean the end of horror and the beginning of something wonderful?"

Oskar pulled off my cap, pushed his hair behind his ears, and wiped off the lipstick. It was obvious, however, that something was wrong. I missed a certain smile on his face. Usually when he returned from a successful mission, he wore a certain self-congratulatory expression because of the triumph he felt (and often talked about) at having once more outwitted his enemies and helped his friends.

"We are smarter than they are," he liked to say. "And in the end, it will be we who win."

This kind of lightheartedness in the face of the constant danger in which he lived made Oskar's company so desirable. Incongruous, but pleasant in a time when fear-ridden faces were all one saw. But right now there was no smile. Oskar was solemn.

"Ilse," he said, "this was torture for me! Being dressed as a girl made me so anxious, so self-conscious, so scared that I'd better not do it again. It was a good idea, and I can't understand that it should affect *me*—who is so used to charades—the way it did . . . but it does."

"Oskar," I interjected, "you needn't be afraid at all. You look extremely convincing in girl's clothing."

"I know," he said. And, not without humor, he told me that a young soldier had tried to pick him up.

He also told me, since I had not left my sector of town for quite some time, that there was not a single part of Berlin that was not in ruins. In ruins and flames. And yet crawling with life. The saddest forms of life: long columns of refugees from the east, harried and sagging with fatigue; columns of captured Russian soldiers, followed by columns of German soldiers, mainly the Volkssturm, consisting of old bitter-faced men dragging their feet and briskly marching fourteen- to sixteen-year-old boys, radiant, most of them, and proud to be able to wear a badly fitting uniform and carry a gun. Scurrying about and mingling with the organized columns were hundreds of civilans, Berliners who had lost their homes a few hours or a few nights ago and were now lugging some of their salvaged goods on makeshift little carts or simply on their backs.

Oskar described it all so vividly I could not bear it anymore.

"Stop, Oskar! Stop it," I said harshly and was ashamed instantly.

Oskar's voice, as always, had remained low and soft.

"All right," Oskar said, "let's change the mood. Let's have a feast! Let's be extravagant and have an opulent dinner. A *whole* tin of sardines! All right? And, should there be a drop of vodka in the house, let's drink a welcome toast to our advancing Russian liberators."

I was, as so often, startled at how quickly Oskar could swing from one mood to another. And since I didn't want to be a spoilsport, I promised to serve the sardines on my best set of china—and conjure up some vodka. To do that, I knocked on my landlady's door, knowing that her friend Bruno would probably have some. I offered butter coupons in exchange for a few ounces of vodka.

"I don't want your butter coupons," Bruno said, "and vodka you can have only if you give us the pleasure of your company for dinner. Will you?" he asked when I hesitated to accept. "You can bring your friend, too. He'll amuse my sister. She will arrive soon, and she loves music.

"Furthermore," he added, "you needn't bring food coupons. I've made a killing: lots of beef. Frau Lasker has prepared a fine stew."

And indeed, the stew was delicious. And the amount of meat was staggering. We were coaxed to eat as much as we wanted and advised to drink plenty of vodka to digest this rich meal, which our stomachs weren't used to anymore.

We didn't talk much while eating, and after we had finished, we were pleasantly drowsy. Bruno's sister, who looked so much like her brother—huge, big-boned, and fat—was the only one still wide awake. She seemed to expect more from a dinner party than just food. She asked Oskar to play a piece or two. But first we thanked Frau Lasker and mainly Bruno, the provider of the large amount of meat. A bit boisterous and rather drunk, he now wanted to hear from each of us how much we had enjoyed the meal. After he had gleaned all our praise, he jumped up from his chair, did a little jig, and burst out laughing.

Then he stopped laughing and neighed.

"Children," he shouted. For several seconds convulsive laughter prevented him from going on. "Children," he gasped, "you have eaten *horse meat*."

Oskar joined Bruno in his nonstop laughter.

Frau Lasker and I shrugged.

But Bruno's sister jumped from her chair, covered her mouth with both hands, and ran as fast as she could to the bathroom.

Thé laughter ceased. We sat quietly, waiting for her return. Minutes passed. She was pale, very pale, when she entered the room.

Without looking at anybody in particular, she said, "Thank you. It was a wonderful meal."

No irony in her voice. No accusation. Nothing. But she did not sit down again. She declared she had to leave.

Oskar got up quickly. "Allow me to take you home," he said and fetched her coat.

Bruno insisted he would take her home.

"I prefer Herr Haupt's company," Bruno's sister said, kissed her brother's cheek lightly, and left on Oskar's arm.

I said a hasty good night to Bruno and Frau Lasker and retreated to my room.

From now on events moved so swiftly night was hardly distinguishable from day. Often the ocean of fire made the nights brighter than the days, during which the dense smoke clouds kept the city in near darkness. Even we who did not, like many Berliners, stay underground lost all sense of time.

April 20, however, Hitler's birthday, we anticipated with great fear. And we got several presents: a five-hour-long Allied bombardment at night and, at five-thirty in the morning, another bombardment from the Russians. In addition, we got double rations on our food coupons, and even two weeks in advance.

Though it was dangerous to expose yourself to the hail of shrapnel, some housewives stood for hours in front of grocery stores. Many were hurt. Some were killed.

The nights, however, became quiet: no Allied bombers anymore. The sky over Berlin seemed to belong to the Russians. They came in daytime, strafing the streets from their low-flying planes. The machine-gun thunder got louder every day. The Russian planes flew so low that the German flak, aiming at them, frequently hit rooftops and set houses on fire.

Bruno and his sister had joined us permanently by now. And there was no electricity anymore, which also meant no water. Luckily I had discovered an old-fashioned water pump in the small garden under the windows of my room. Against the stern warnings of everybody, I put a heavy cooking pot on my head, climbed out the window, and returned with two buckets full of water.

I was treated like a hero. Oskar promised me the Iron Cross. Now we could have hot coffee. Real coffee, another of Hitler's birthday presents, and we could also heat up some soup on our little spirit stove.

We were in the middle of our meal when I went to answer a knock on the hall door.

A boy stood in front of me. A child really, clad in a rumpled uniform much too big for his skinny body, clutching a bazooka.

"Pardon me," he said, "could I have a glass of water?"

I nodded, let him in, and fetched the water.

"You're lucky," I said, "half an hour ago I wouldn't have had any water." And I told him how I got it.

"Let me get some more for you," he pleaded.

"All right," I said, "that would be nice. But first . . . it seems to me you need a little rest."

"Do I?" he asked, pulling back his sagging shoulders, trying to stand straight and tall.

I led him into my room and set him down on my couch. I encouraged him to lie down. He took off his heavy, dirty shoes and put the bazooka on the floor beside them.

"I'm in the Volkssturm," he declared.

Did I hear pride or defiance in his voice? I wasn't sure.

"Gunter Muller is my name," he said. "I'm thirteen-and-a-half years old."

I told him to call me Ilse.

As soon as he was on his back, he fell asleep, snoring. I stood awhile beside him, studying his face: a milky, soft, child's face. Though deep in sleep, he tossed frequently and muttered words not understandable. Once I thought I heard him say Mama.

I left the room and joined Oskar, who had stayed out of sight in the kitchen. We decided to remain there and let our young soldier have a couple of hours of sleep.

When we woke him, he jerked up like a jack-in-the-box and looked around, bewildered.

"It's all right," I said soothingly.

He rubbed his eyes and slowly seemed to remember where he was. Then panic overcame him.

"They'll hang me!" he blurted out. "They'll hang me as a deserter and a traitor."

"No, no, no," I said. "Nobody knows you're here."

But, still panic-stricken, he told us that he had seen many German soldiers, young and old, strung up on lampposts and trees.

"No such danger for you," Oskar comforted. "You'll take off

that ugly uniform and slip into a pair of my trousers and a sweater. That will save you."

"Will it?" Gunter asked, frowning, but a slight smile flicked over his face.

"How did you get here?" Oskar asked him.

And Gunter told how he had lost his unit during a fight with Russian tanks.

"The Russian tanks shot at us point blank," he said, "killing most of our unit. But I ran. I ran without thinking, without knowing where I was running to, without any goal or sense of direction. Terror just drove me on."

"For how long did you run?"

"I don't know. Fifteen minutes or twenty. I really don't know."

"Do you remember where this encounter with the Russian tanks took place? It can't be very far from here."

"It was at the Tiergarten, close to the Brandenburg Gate, I think."

Oskar and I exchanged glances. We knew the gate was not more than three or four miles away.

"Most of my comrades were very brave," Gunter went on, "but I'm not." In a whisper he added, "I ran."

"Good for you," Oskar said.

Gunter's questioning eyes went from Oskar's face to mine.

"Well," he said, "I don't know . . . maybe we could have stopped the Russians from entering Berlin. Goebbels said we could. Our love for the Führer and our desire to protect him would give us courage and strength to fight to the last man. That's what Goebbels said."

"And did it?" I asked. "Did the love for the Führer help your comrades to be brave? And what about you?"

"Well," Gunter replied, "my love for the Führer isn't that

great. But I would have liked to protect the people, the Berliners. My mother, my sister, and many of my friends are still in Berlin. I would have liked to prevent Berlin from becoming a battlefield. However, for many of my comrades, Goebbels's fiery speech worked, and they were extremely brave. They stepped so close to the Russian tanks, they could fire their bazookas and most of the time blow them up."

"And what happened," I wanted to know, "when the tank was not blown up?"

Gunter shrugged.

"What happened?" I urged.

"*They* were blown up. I've seen them lying in puddles of blood." He turned his face to the wall and wiped off a tear.

"Now I'll get you more water," he said and, trying to sound cheerful, he added, "For that I'm still brave enough."

He went back and forth to the pump until all the containers we could find were filled.

Gratefully and silently he shared our evening meal. Later that night, he lay down to sleep beside Oskar on a bed of cushions I had improvised on the floor.

The following morning, Oskar and Gunter discussed the danger the gasoline tank in front of our door presented. They tried to move it, but, of course, they could not. It was much too heavy.

We stayed inside during the day, and our young soldier sat quietly in a corner, brooding. I had some cleanup work to do. Whenever a house nearby was hit, our walls shook and mortar dust and plaster chips fell from the ceiling. And, though in "normal times" a light layer of dust on my furniture didn't bother me at all, I now had a strong desire to keep my immediate surroundings as clean as possible.

Sometimes I took refuge in reading. Rilke and Goethe took me to another level of existence—for a short time at least.

Oskar, playing his recorder, also helped to banish reality. He seemed to be the one least changed: he had not lost his resilience. After playing for hours, which we all loved, he also talked. And when he talked, he did not speak of the present or the future. He remembered a summer afternoon he had spent on the beach at the Wannsee. Though it was a weekday, he told us, the beach was crowded. Workers had been given the afternoon off so they could hear an announced "important" speech by Goebbels. Many people, just like Oskar, must have wanted to escape Goebbels's tirade and had come to enjoy the beach instead. Oskar had spread his blanket and had just settled down when a man close to him turned on his radio. After boastful statements about Hitler's success and glory in general, Goebbels came to the crux of his speech: He introduced the Volkswagen! "The miracle car of the century," he called it. "This car will conquer the world," Goebbels declared, his voice trembling with emotion. Tremendous applause followed.

Oskar had soon lost interest in the speech and watched a motorboat racing across a wide stretch of sparkling water. After circling several times, the boat steered toward the shore and anchored a few yards from where Oskar sat. A young man and a young woman helped four children out of the boat and led them to the beach. Blankets were spread out and a food basket put down. The children, obviously hungry, wanted to eat. The pretty, super-blond young woman, clearly not their mother, paid no attention to them.

Instead she let the young man light her cigarette, puffed a few smoke clouds in his face, smiled a toothy smile, and leaned her head on his shoulder. The children, trying to open the basket by themselves, were harshly reprimanded: "Keep your hands off!" "I'm so thirsty," one child whimpered. "Later" was all the young woman said. By now she had coaxed the young man to lie down, and from her hand filled with sand, she let a trickle run through her fingers onto his naked chest.

Why did the children look so familiar? Oskar had suddenly wondered. And it took him only a few moments to recognize them: the Goebbels children! They had come from their nearby home on the Schwanenwerda peninsula.

Poor rich children, Oskar had thought, and he walked away from the Goebbels speech and the Goebbels children.

The days that followed were endless and yet they seemed to blend together as if they were just one long day of misery.

We stayed inside, waited, and listened. For hours it was deathly quiet. Then, for half an hour, we heard the strafing Russian airplanes and the stutter of machine guns. The falling shrapnel sounded like hail.

Whenever a shell exploded nearby, Oskar grinned fiendishly and said, "They haven't hit us yet."

The radio had been silent for several days. The last newscast we heard was on April 22 when Goebbels informed us that the Führer was in Berlin and would die fighting with his troops defending the capital city. This had ended the many rumors and speculations about Hitler's whereabouts. Since the last time the Germans had heard Hitler's voice on the radio had been January 30, many thought, or hoped, he was dead.

Surprisingly, telephones still functioned—at least most of the time. I tried to reach an aunt of mine living in the northeastern part of the city. My shock was great when a Russian voice answered. I was so stunned that I hung up instantly. Thinking I had misdialed, I dialed again. The same Russian voice answered.

After all of us had stayed indoors for days in a row, the tension grew. The thunder of the frequent artillery bombardments, which came without warning, the long silences in between, all this was different from the Allied air attacks we had gotten used to. We did not know what to make of it.

"I'll go and look," I declared during a lull, and nobody could hold me back.

With a gossamer scarf tightly wrapped around my head to protect me from smoke and floating cinders, a cooking pot in my hand to function, if need be, as a helmet, I stepped into the street.

The street was empty.

I looked toward the corner where Meinekestrasse crossed Lietzenburgerstrasse. There was a throng of agitated people in front of a grocery store. I was surprised, since days before a sign on the door had said: Closed Due to Lack of Water and Electricity.

I went to find out what was going on. The entrance was smashed open. The inside was packed full with women grabbing whatever they could reach, fighting with each other over packages and cans, tearing and clawing sacks of flour, sugar, beans, and rice from one another's hands until some sacks broke open and spilled their contents on the floor. As I watched this plundering from the outside, I was pushed by people behind me into the store. I saw women stepping on one another's shoulders to reach the high shelves. One woman, her arms loaded, lost her balance and fell against the edge of a metal shelf. Blood streaming from her forehead, her lips squeezed tightly shut, she went on grabbing item after item.

I was ashamed for all of them. Even more so for myself when I, fighting my way out, took a can of tuna and slipped it in my pocket. What right did I have to judge these women so harshly, I asked myself. Maybe they had starving children at home.

I took a turn around the next block. It looked like everywhere else: rows and rows of roofless houses. Deep craters, often filled with filthy water, next to mountains of rubble over which it was difficult to climb. Every once in a while, during a lull in the shelling, some people dared to creep out of their basement shelters to check what was going on.

They stopped me, asking, "Some news?"

I shook my head.

"We heard the Russians are plundering and raping everywhere," a young woman shouted.

"We heard the Bolshevik hordes will be stopped by the Volkssturm and the Home Guard," another one added.

Suddenly there was the shutter of machine guns. A single low-flying Russian plane was directly over us, and bullets crashed against the walls. Hastily the people withdrew to their basements.

I put the cooking pot on my head and hurried on. Seconds later it was quiet again.

The next street, Uhlandstrasse, was likewise a sad sight. On what once had been a broad thoroughfare, I had now to tread warily on a narrow path winding through mountains of rubble. Once I had to climb over an enormous stone figure of a woman, a caryatid. She had broken off from an ornate portal that had graced the entrance to a house of the kind so frequent in Berlin-West. They had been built shortly before the turn of the century. Built solidly to last for centuries to come.

Here and there, people, their faces blackened by smoke and

cinders, scratched in the ashes of burned-out houses, hoping to find something of their belongings that might have survived the fire.

I turned right into the Kurfürstendamm and had to let a column of German soldiers pass. They were not marching anymore; they were dragging their feet. Some were limping, some had bloody bandages on their heads, their faces ashen and fear-ridden.

Before the officer, in not much better condition than the column he led, pushed me aside, I asked one of the soldiers, "Where are you going?"

"From one front to another," he answered and, with a short, scornful laugh, he added, "which means from West to East Berlin."

A right turn again, and I entered Meinekestrasse. Approaching my house I saw an elderly man in an S.A. uniform swing a broad brush and write in big white letters BERLIN WILL REMAIN GERMAN on a wall. And number twenty-one, my house, proclaimed WHO BELIEVES IN HITLER BELIEVES IN VICTORY. I would have liked to ask the spreader of such news how many people, he thought, still believed in Hitler. But, of course, I didn't.

Returning home I had to report in detail on what I had seen. With a mixture of pride and shame, I showed my trophy, the can of stolen tuna. "We will make a feast of it," I promised.

Our Gunter had listened attentively. Most of the three days he had spent with us, he had sat nearly motionless in a corner, hardly uttering a word. But now a change came over him.

He jumped from his chair and declared, "I have to leave. My mother, my sisters . . . they live just a few miles from here. They will need me."

So much determination was in his voice that neither Oskar

nor I tried to hold him back. Wanting to do something for him, I opened the stolen can, and with a tuna sandwich and our blessings we let him go.

He was so moved at the last handshake that he could only stammer, "Thank you."

"Look," Oskar said when we were back in my room, "look, Gunter has left us something to remember him by." He pointed to the bazooka lying under Gunter's chair. "I'll get rid of it as soon as it gets dark."

"No," I said, "*I* will."

A while after Gunter left, I began to feel guilty. I should have tried to hold him back. He should not be walking the streets. In a way I felt responsible for this youth: so lost, so helpless.

Oskar tried to comfort me. "I took his papers away. We must burn them now."

"A young man without papers?" I asked, horrified.

"Better than being a proven deserter by having papers," Oskar said.

Gunter must have returned briefly a short time after leaving because I found a scrap of paper pushed under the hall door. It read, I will return the trousers and the sweater as soon as possible.

I could not stop thinking of Gunter. And my feeling of guilt grew and extended: I thought of my parents. They lived about sixty miles southeast of Berlin, in Silesia, which must have been already overrun by the Russians. Where were they now? Did they stay in their house east of the Neisse river? Or did they flee? And if so, where did they flee? Shouldn't I have gone to help them? Even in normal times my mother was a woman whose vivid imagination (leaning to the dark side of life) often overwhelmed her. How would she hold up now when horror and disaster were reality? It was a slight comfort, however, to think of my father.

He, the extreme opposite of Mother, would arrange everything as prudently as possible.

When night came, I took the bazooka, carried it as tenderly as if it were a baby to the next ruin, and set it gently down.

Returning, I could not resist walking up the four flights to the attic and then stepping out on the roof. The city stretched out below me as I had never seen it before. The heavy smoke clouds above were aglow with the reflections of the raging fires on the ground. Whole blocks of houses burning here and there. Black areas in between, probably buildings demolished long ago. I had hoped to see a line of artillery fire somewhere toward the east, defining the front line the Russians were holding. But no such line was visible. Instead there was artillery fire scattered all round me, some of it very close. It was obvious the Russians were all over the city, some only a stone's throw from Meinekestrasse.

I was tempted to fetch Oskar. To him this sight would have revealed more than it did to me. But he couldn't be on the roof, where at any moment the house firewarden might appear.

I went down and found Oskar in Frau Lasker's room, where the four of them seemed to have made it their goal to empty a bottle of schnapps.

"Come, Ilse," Bruno said. "Help us finish the schnapps. It should not fall into the hands of our liberators."

I joined them. Already with the second drink, I pushed the grim picture I had seen from the rooftop into the background. Oh, what a comfort liquor was in times like these. After the third glass, I didn't even mind Bruno's rough manners and speech anymore. We stayed up, drinking and talking, until the early-morning hours.

"Great," Bruno exclaimed, "no sirens anymore. No heavy bombardments."

"Only a few friendly Russian shells," Oskar said, grinning.

"How grateful we have to be that our house still stands," said Frau Lasker.

We all agreed and drank to this.

"When will they be here?" Bruno's sister asked timidly. "To be honest, I would have liked the British or the Americans to come first. The Russians are supposed to—"

Bruno interrupted. "You needn't be afraid of being raped, you fat old bag," he said while smacking a loud kiss on her cheek. "It's different though with Ilse," he continued, "and also with my lady. We will have to smear their faces with ashes. That's what we will have to do."

"I'm not afraid of the Russians," I said. "Most of the horror stories we hear will turn out to be just Goebbels's propaganda."

"I hope you are right," Bruno's sister murmured.

After Oskar and I, with hot and dizzy heads, had retreated to my room, I suddenly felt the desire to step outside for a moment. Not into the street but to the small garden below my window where I had fetched water.

"Let's climb out the window and get a breath of fresh air," I proposed.

Oskar laughed mockingly. "Fresh air? Outdoors? You seem to be living in the good old days of five years ago."

"Well," I said, "just a bit of grass under my feet will do. After all, it's spring."

I opened the window, jumped out, and coaxed Oskar to follow me. It must have rained a little and since there had not been a fire in our immediate neighborhood during the last few days, the odor of the sprouting grass and the soft, thawed earth was stronger than the smell of ashes and cinders we were so used to.

We enjoyed stepping on the resilient earth and splashing cold water from the pump on our liquor-heated faces.

But dawn was breaking and with it the artillery fire got stronger. When we heard airplanes approaching, we quickly climbed back into my room.

We lay down, hoping for a little sleep—fully dressed, of course. For several nights we had not gotten out of our clothes. We kept a small suitcase with a change of clothes and a few cans of food close by. Just in case.

I woke up shortly before noon when Oskar offered me a sip of tea Frau Lasker had brewed.

"The artillery fire is extremely heavy today," Oskar told me. "Also very close," he added.

I listened. For the moment it was quiet. But suddenly I heard another sound. Was it the grunting of animals? The growling of bears? Oskar and I held our breath. The sound got louder and turned into shouting. And then it dawned on us: Russian voices. The guttural sounds typical of eastern European tongues.

And through the small piece of glass set into the cardboard covering my window, we looked out into the garden and saw three Russian soldiers trying to overcome four Volkssturm soldiers.

"That's it," Oskar said, matter-of-factly.

But my heart beat like a drum. My knees trembled, and for seconds I could hardly move.

Oskar went to tell Frau Lasker and her friends, who were not yet aware of what was going on. We all crowded into the corridor, trying to make up our minds what to do.

And then it happened: a tremendous concussion shook the

walls. And what followed was Niagara Falls! Something I had never heard before: a thundering, rushing sound as if masses of water were falling to a deep depth. Niagara Falls, that was all I could think of. Niagara Falls directly beyond the door that separated our corridor from the main entrance hall. A second later, before we could grasp what had happened, burning gasoline flowed from under the door into our corridor.

"The gasoline tank was hit," Oskar, still calm, explained. "Out! We must get out immediately. We can't take anything with us. We have *seconds* only."

I grabbed my fur coat, which hung within reach, and my pocketbook, which, luckily, hung beside it. I couldn't fetch the small emergency suitcase because the door to my room was in flames. Everybody reached for what was near and ran along the corridor to Frau Lasker's bedroom. Its single window faced the courtyard that separated the garden house from the front house, where the air-raid shelter was. We climbed through the window and crossed the courtyard, in which man-to-man fighting between Russian and German soldiers raged.

I ran as fast as the turmoil allowed, not looking right or left. Bullets hissed past my ears. Howling and ear-shattering screams echoed from the walls enclosing the courtyard. I could not see any of the others. Had they reached the shelter before me?

I was just at the entrance to the basement when, over the din of shooting and shouting, I heard a desperate cry: "Help me! Help me!"

I looked back and saw Bruno's sister, huge and clumsy as she was, stuck in the window, trying to get out. I hesitated only a second before crossing the courtyard again to free her. Her overcoat was caught on a protruding bolt in the window frame. I pulled her loose and, ducking, shoved her through the ongoing fight till we reached the basement door. There she fell into the arms of her brother, who was standing at the entrance, looking for her.

The shelter was filled to capacity. It was dark. I couldn't see anything and wondered how I would find Oskar when a hand reached for mine.

"Thank goodness you are here, Ilse," Oskar said. "I was just going out again to look for you."

I clung to his hand while we slowly fought our way through the throng of people, pressed together out of fear or because of lack of space.

"Let's find a corner," Oskar suggested.

We did and squatted down.

The moment I sat down I collapsed. All my strength left me, and I began to tremble and shake. Oskar put his arm around me, but I could not stop shaking. I didn't know where I was. The cacophony of voices seemed to come from far away—the bottom of the ocean, maybe. It did not feel as if I were still on Mother Earth.

It took some time until I got hold of myself.

And then I became aware of the whining, the praying, the cursing around me. Some people, drunk it seemed, sang frivolous songs; others, church songs and hymns. Some people declared their determination to survive. To survive by all means. While others called for death to redeem them.

Minute after minute it got hotter in the basement. It became unbearable, and almost everybody began tearing off their clothing. Smoke filtered in. Coughing began slowly and increased to un-interrupted coughing fits.

Somebody lit a candle and was ordered harshly by Bruno, who had taken command of this "sinking ship," as he put it, to blow it out. "We need every ounce of oxygen."

Then Bruno stepped to the wooden door leading to the anteroom of our shelter, touched it, and announced, "It's getting damn hot!"

His next command was to call all the men to the door and order them to urinate against it.

From outside only muffled sounds penetrated the heavy walls fortified with sandbags. We did not know what was going on out there.

When the smoke got so intense that death by suffocation seemed imminent, Oskar, who had discovered a door leading out of the basement toward the street, declared he would go and see if it was possible to get out and flee to another house. I wanted to hold him back. I was afraid I would never see him again.

But he left and returned quickly. He had, for a moment only, opened the door a slit. There was heavy fighting in the street in front of our house.

"Not much chance of getting through alive," he said.

He had also seen that the fire from the garden house had spread to the front house.

He sat down beside me. The smoke had gotten so thick I could hardly see his face.

"Now," I said, putting my cyanide capsule in Oskar's hand.

"No," he said.

"What then?" I asked.

"This," he said, pulling his recorder from his pocket.

A Bach fugue hushed the din in the basement for just a second. Then the howling and praying resumed.

Trying to suppress my coughing, I leaned my head against

Oskar's shoulder. Our death song, I thought. And for a moment I wanted to pray. But to whom? To God? To Buddha? To Jehovah? And for what? I was in such inner turmoil that I decided to try not to think at all. However, that was not possible. The desirable state of nothingness, of nirvana, that I once had hoped to acquire from Buddhism, did not work for me. Instead I was plagued by the thought . . . that I had no thoughts at all. Wasn't your whole life supposed to flash through your mind just before death? For me, it didn't. And love? Was love still inside me? For my mother, my father, and, most of all, my grandmother? Yes! Will I be united with her in heaven? Or will I sit on a lotus flower? And if I died and yet had a chance to tell somebody how it was to die, what would I tell?

Thought splinters like this went through my mind. Then nothingness again. No despair. No hope. And yet nothing resembling the blessed feeling of nirvana.

Oskar's music? Yes . . . it felt good.

"Let's open the cyanide now," I said.

"No," Oskar said. He put away his recorder. "I'll check once more what's going on outdoors."

He'll never be back, I thought. He will be shot. And I will die alone. Surrounded by a hundred people and yet alone. And while waiting for that moment, a thought—no, rather a feeling—took hold of me. A guilty secret that had gnawed on me for years. Never had I talked about it to anybody, but often I had sat in judgment on myself. Sometimes I came out a criminal; at other, more forgiving times, a rescuing angel, a redeemer.

It had happened three years ago. I had gone home for the Christmas holidays. I knew that my grandmother, who was the most beloved and important person in my life, had been severely ill for several months. She was over eighty, and in spite of good care by my mother and a doctor who came every day, she got worse and worse. I was shattered when I saw how much more frail she had become since the last time I had seen her. She was without pain for a few short hours only when the few drops of morphine the doctor had prescribed were effective. When the morphine wore off, she was still in a daze, but moaning and whimpering steadily.

For three days I sat at her bedside, caressing her bony hands. Most of the time her eyes were closed and she did not seem to be aware of my presence. But once in a while she opened her eyes, and a faint smile flickered over her face.

"Ilselein, my Ilselein," she would then whisper, recognizing me for a moment only.

One day, with a pain-tortured face I heard her mutter, "The war, the war."

I bent over her and said, "The war is over now."

Then—and I will never forget it—she opened her eyes wide. She looked at me for a long time and said, "But Ilselein, you have never lied to me before." I turned my head so she wouldn't see my tears.

When the doctor came, I asked him whether her pains couldn't be reduced. He shrugged but finally increased the amount of morphine to be given her at night.

"Is there any hope to cure her?" I asked.

He said she was over eighty, and the many afflictions she suffered from were beyond a cure.

Three extremely difficult days followed. Her moaning turned to screams. Her body was shaken by strange powers within her. Where did she get the strength from, I wondered. She had taken only liquids for many days.

Then, suddenly, between screams, she whispered, "Death. *Sweet* death." I took her in my arms. "Come," she said.

When night arrived—it was Christmas Eve—I knew what I had to do. And I did it. Instead of the prescribed drops of morphine, I gave her half the bottle. I sat with her until she fell asleep. But not, like the preceding nights, did I sleep on a cot in her room.

Instead I went downstairs to a room that years ago had been my playroom. It was a long night during which I did not sleep. I waited for the morning and for my mother to come and tell me that grandmother had died peacefully during the night. It was far into the morning when Mother finally came.

"Our Dodo," she said, "has had a good, long sleep last night. She seems to feel better and is more quiet . . . Why are you crying?"

I left the day after Christmas. My grandmother died on New Year's Eve.

And now, sitting in this dark, smoke-filled, hellish room, death staring me in the face, I would have liked to tell someone, Oskar, and hear his verdict.

But when Oskar was suddenly beside me again there was no time because Oskar, raising his voice, commanded, "Silence!"

I didn't know Oskar's voice could become so loud.

"Silence!" he shouted again. "I've checked the street. The heavy fighting is far away, at the corner of Lietzenburgerstrasse. There's only a skirmish, just a handful of soldiers, fighting in front of our house. We could try to get through and run to the house across the street, which is still unharmed."

A short silence followed this offer to escape certain death.

"You call Lietzenburgerstrasse far away?" someone grumbled.

Oskar paid no attention. "Let's go!" he shouted. "No time to lose!"

He took me by the hand and led me to the door. A long column of people followed us. We stepped outside, our heads pulled in, looking down to avoid stepping on ammunition strewn on the ground. With German and Russian soldiers fighting all around us, we stumbled our way to the house across the street. Not everybody made it. Some were hit by bullets not aimed at them.

But Oskar and I did.

The reception our crowd got pushing into the shelter was not a friendly one.

"We are filled up," declared the air-raid warden, guarding the entrance like a Cerberus. "You can't get in here."

As Oskar explained our situation, we were pushed so hard by the people behind that the air-raid warden could not stand up against us. Slowly we were shoved into the basement which, indeed, was already overcrowded. We had to endure all kinds of curses. But there were also some kind voices, and some people moved closer together to make room for the newcomers.

This air shelter was not one large space as ours had been. It was a labyrinth of nooks and niches filled with people nestling together. There were very few men, mainly women and a few children. Thousands of children had been evacuated long ago, leaving anxious mothers behind. Quarrels and fights broke out all around us. One woman, lighting a cigarette, was not only attacked by words, but also by fists. Some people shoved others aside to make more room for themselves, to be able to stretch out.

But to me it all seemed rather subdued compared to the pandemonium we had escaped from.

As new arrivals, we were overwhelmed with questions. Many people, afraid of the shelling, had been living underground for longer than a week, and they wanted to know how many houses in our block were still standing. Different people reacted differently to the news that the Russians were fighting in our street. Some rejoiced, saying the war would be over within an hour. Others panicked and retold the monstrous reports the Propaganda Ministry had spread about the "Jewish-Bolshevik pigs."

Oskar and I, among the first to enter the shelter, were pushed in deep by those who followed. But now Oskar insisted we should work our way back to the entrance.

"There we will get a whiff of air once in a while when the door is opened," he said. "And I can peek out and keep an eye on what is happening outside."

It took us nearly an hour to make our way to the door. And there I stood, aimless and helpless, elbow to elbow with strangers, when I felt a tug on my coat.

An old woman got up from the floor. "Come, children," she said, "I can sit on my suitcase. That will make enough room for the young man to sit down and let you sit on his lap."

I thanked the old lady, and we did as she suggested.

Our eyes slowly adjusted to the darkness. Spread far apart were a few petrol lamps, and the faces of the people within the small circle of their light were lifted out of the darkness as if they belonged to actors on a stage. The whole scale of dark emotions was reflected in them: horror, fear, helplessness, fatigue, and resignation.

I closed my eyes.

The old woman beside me began to hum. It was the melody of a long-forgotten childhood song. It told about an elderberry bush . . . that bloomed so beautifully in the month of May.

"It is May first today, isn't it?" she asked.

"Yes," Oskar replied, and added, "unfortunately."

"Oh, yes," she said, "it's the Russians' big holiday."

"Indeed it is," said Oskar, "and it will not do us much good."

"I know, I know," the old woman sighed. "Liquor will flow."

A moment later I felt her hand reach for mine. A cool, skinny hand caressed mine lightly.

"I'll try to protect you, child," she said. "When the Russians come, I mean. I'm sure that some of them will rape. How could it be otherwise? But I speak Russian. I will speak to them."

I opened my eyes and tried to make out her face. I couldn't see much. Only that her wide cheekbones gave her a slightly Slavic look. And—I didn't know whether I willed myself to see what I yearned to see or if what I saw was true: she resembled ever so slightly my beloved grandmother.

I told her that I knew a little Russian, too, and that I wasn't afraid of them.

Oskar, who did not feel comfortable with me on his lap, asked me to stand up so he could get up.

"I'll go and look for Frau Lasker and company," he said.

He left, and I let my old lady friend sit down again in the space she had vacated for Oskar and me. I sat down on her suitcase. We spent some time practicing Russian, and I learned a few more words and phrases.

Then Oskar returned. He had found Frau Lasker and Bruno and his sister huddled together, overcome by fear. He could not persuade them to join us. They wanted to be as far away as possible from the door through which they expected the Russians to enter at any moment.

"Do you have anything to eat?" the old lady asked.

"No," I said, "but it doesn't matter."

A moment later she put a zwieback into my hand. "And here's one more for your man."

I didn't want to accept, but she insisted. Oskar and I decided to share one and save the other for later.

All of a sudden the little old lady was asleep. Her head swayed back and forth. I pulled it onto my lap, and now I hummed the song of the elderberry bush, thinking of my grandmother. So often in my childhood she had sung me to sleep with this song.

The snoring all around us told me it was night.

"Try to sleep," suggested Oskar, who by now had squatted down at my feet.

"Impossible," I said, but I urged him to sleep.

"By no means," he replied. "The Russians can enter this basement at any moment. I've checked. There's no fighting anymore. Only groups of drunken Russians in the street, dragging all kinds of stuff—lamps, suitcases, chairs, clocks, and radios—out of the houses still standing."

The night seemed endless. Oskar, who surprisingly had befriended the rough air-raid warden, was now allowed to stand beside him at the entrance door and take a peek in the street every so often. Late at night he told me the situation had not changed much: The Russians seemed to be celebrating. They were hollering, laughing, and singing. He had even seen a German girl linking arms with two Russians. She, too, was singing and laughing.

Morning came. The little old lady woke up with a smile. She had dreamed of a birch grove, she told me, surrounded by a flower-strewn meadow, the air pungent with the scent of mushrooms and filled with larks who, as she put it, were climbing on their songs into the sky.

Then she whispered in my ear: "Such were the mornings of my childhood . . . in Russia."

I couldn't help but kiss her.

We were munching on our zwieback when the entrance door was pushed open with a crash, letting in the morning light.

But instantly the light was cut off by a large figure, filling the door frame: a Russian soldier with a gun slung over his shoulder and a pistol in his left hand.

The din in the basement changed to churchlike quiet.

Then the soldier unbuttoned his heavy long overcoat and, with a strangely measured gesture, which made me think of a mannequin, he opened the right side of it, revealing an uncountable number of wristwatches. They were safety-pinned in rows to the inside of his coat, starting at the top and going down to the bottom. But that wasn't all. He shifted the pistol from his left hand and flung open the left side of his coat, likewise covered with wristwatches.

A proud, childlike smile lit up his face under the high fur cap.

The smile faded quickly. He stepped forward, pushing his way through the crowd.

"Urri, urri!" he shouted.

It took me a moment to realize *urri, urri* meant *Uhren*, watches.

It obviously was an order. When nobody obeyed, he reached for the arm of a woman, pulled the watch off her wrist, said *dunke*, and turned immediately to the next person for the next watch.

"If all we lose is a wristwatch," Oskar said, "it's all right."

Soon more Russians arrived, and they weren't quite as "polite" as the first one had been. When their demand for *urri, urri* was not instantly fulfilled, they pulled their pistols out and shot. At first at the ceiling. One, however, obviously very drunk, didn't raise his pistol high enough and several shots went into the crowd.

Heartrending screams, moaning, blood spurting, corpses.

And now wave after wave of Russian soldiers arrived. And since they could not get enough *urri* anymore, they began to rape.

They did not discriminate between young and old. They did not care whether their prey was eight or eighty. Layer by layer they tore the clothes from their victims, threw them on the floor, and did their business.

I, up to now, had lost only my watch, but in the ensuing commotion I had been separated from my Russian lady friend. Desperately I tried to get back to her. I found her. She was slumped over her suitcase, a trickle of blood oozing from her mouth, her eyes staring at the ceiling.

As I bent down to close her eyes, I was forcefully jerked up and pushed against a wall. A Russian who seemed a bit older than most of the others tried to pull down my slacks. I cried for Oskar, but he was nowhere in sight.

The Russian put his hand over my mouth and at that moment, when I thought there was no hope of escaping anymore, something happened, something clicked inside me, and I decided *not* to try to fight him off or run away. I had observed that those women who did just that seemed to arouse the hunting instinct in their pursuer even more, and they were treated the worst.

So I did just the opposite: I flung my arms around my attacker's neck, pressed my body against his, looked into his eyes and, smiling, stammered my well-rehearsed little welcome speech in Russian.

The effect was enormous. His hands, still holding me in a forceful grip, fell to his sides. He took a step backward and looked at me in disbelief.

"So glad you come liberate," I said.

He stared.

"Long wait," I continued. "Now Hitler kaput. You here. Everything good."

"You speak Russian," he said, astonished. It was not a

question, but a statement. He shook his head, removed his fur cap, and scratched his head. He was bewildered.

He even seemed helpless when I went on speaking Russian, humbly apologizing that my Russian was not so good. "Beautiful but difficult language," I said.

"Deutschlandsprache auch schwer," German also difficult, he said in German, mispronouncing every word.

But I told him his German sounded fine, though he should try to emphasize the first instead of the second syllable of the word *Deutschland*. He nodded and tried over and over again until we both laughed.

Oskar had joined us, watching this scene with amusement.

"This husband," I told my Russian conquest. "Speaks no Russian. But *good* husband."

Oskar's admiring glances and his whispered "You're doing great, Ilse" made me so audacious that I added, "He good father, too."

"Aaah! Children?" the Russian said. He seemed delighted and slapped his thighs.

"Yes," I said, "four."

"Where?" he asked.

"Evacuated," I answered. "Out of city."

Our conversation halted when we heard shooting again.

"I go stop that," said our Russian.

He left us, fought his way through the agitated crowd to where the shots had come from. Minutes later he dragged two Russian soldiers, holding them by their necks, out of the shelter.

He returned to us. "Me go now," he explained, "duty."

But he hesitated and looked at Oskar and me—from head to toe.

"You thin," he said. "You no eat?"

We shrugged.

"Will come later. Bring bread, sausage. All right?"

And indeed, with a loaf of black bread and a large piece of sausage, he returned half an hour later.

He also brought more. "Good news!" he announced. "Shooting no more! Berlin kaput—capitulated!"

"We victory," he added radiantly. "You go street now. Me work to do."

I had no time to construct a proper Russian thank-you sentence. I just kissed him on both unshaven cheeks.

He waved good-bye and left.

Greedily Oskar and I devoured the bread and sausage, but the many hungry eyes watching us reduced the pleasure of eating. And when a skinny little boy snatched a piece of bread from my mouth and was scolded by his likewise skinny mother, I broke the bread and sausage in half and handed it to her.

Oskar went out to check and when he came back, he said, "It's true. It really *is* over! Cars are cruising the streets with loudspeakers announcing that today, May second, Berlin has capitulated."

"And our house?" I asked.

"Gone," Oskar said.

"The Kolbe angel too?" I knew it was silly to ask this question.

"Of course!" Oskar said.

Time and again Oskar had to repeat the news about the surrender to all and everybody in the shelter. Now that this long-hoped-for moment had come, people seemed unable to believe it.

Then they began to speculate and asked Oskar if he thought it safe to leave the basement.

"Well, there are a lot of Russians in the streets, drunk and wild with the joy of victory. And every once in a while you can hear a shot being fired." To more, Oskar didn't commit himself.

To me, he said, "I want to leave. I understand if you want to stay. I'll be back before night."

But I was as eager as he to get out. I slipped into my coat, threw my handbag over my shoulder, and followed Oskar, who was already outside.

My first glance went across the street to number twenty-one. Both the front house and the garden house were skeletons: ashes still smoldering, here and there flames still leaping from the ashes. The houses to the right and left were gone, too. But a little further away, toward the Kurfürstendamm, most houses were intact but for broken windows and shrapnel scars. White bed sheets of surrender hung from their facades.

In less than a minute we reached the Kurfürstendamm. Out of a half-demolished building, once an elegant hotel and restaurant, Russians with armloads of bottles emerged. They cracked the bottles open by smashing the necks against the curb and, holding them high above their heads, poured the contents into their mouths.

"Sure," Oskar said, "the wine cellar must be stuffed with liquor stolen from all corners of the world."

There were no civilians in the street. For the first ten minutes we didn't meet a single one. Only long columns of captured German soldiers, escorted by Russian soldiers, moved slowly along the street. Walking wasn't easy because the Kurfürstendamm could hardly be called a street anymore. Bomb craters had formed deep valleys, and houses, fallen into the street, had become mountains strewn with Russian and German corpses.

I wasn't quite prepared for a sight like this. I lowered my head, reached for Oskar's hand, and walked with closed eyes. It worked

for a few minutes, but then I stumbled and nearly fell. I obeyed
Oskar's order to open my eyes and watch where I was stepping.

I turned back to see what had made me stumble. It was an
arm. An arm clad in a blood-soaked black sleeve with the S.S.
emblem on it.

And while I looked, a dog approached, took the arm in his
mouth, and dragged the loot into a ruin. Oskar laughed a bitter
laugh. I had to fight back tears.

Here and there were still nests of resistance. Shots were fired
out of a window.

A Russian officer, at the head of a column of prisoners, stopped.
Through a loudspeaker he ordered, "Come out or the house will
be blown up." Within minutes a dozen German soldiers emerged,
throwing their weapons away and crossing their arms over their
heads. They were handcuffed and made to walk in front of the
Russian officer.

"Where are we going?" I asked Oskar.

"To the Nollendorfplatz," he replied. "I want to see whether
Karl and his girl came through all right."

We passed the Gedächtniskirche (Kaiser-Wilhelm Memorial
Church) and turned into the Tauntzienstrasse. The same picture
of destruction: houses still in flames, and acrid smoke that burned
our throats and hindered our sight.

The corpse of a small crocodile that must have escaped from
the nearby zoo drew Oskar's attention. And a few steps further
on we found a beautiful dead flamingo.

When we reached Wittenbergplatz, we saw what seemed to
be a large amount of people, civilians, who, with bent backs, were
wresting and clawing at something on the ground that we could
not see.

When we came closer, we saw it was a large dead horse. The people, some with pocket knives, some with their bare hands, were tearing piece after piece from the cadaver.

One woman, her arms bloody up to her elbows, triumphantly announced, "I got the heart!" And she devoured it on the spot.

I wanted to pass as quickly as possible, but Oskar held me back.

"Goya would have done justice to this scene," he said.

Oskar was fascinated. I was horrified.

Finally I pried him loose, and we continued our walk. We were thankful that little attention was paid to us by the Russians. But shortly before we reached Karl's apartment house, we were stopped. A Russian stepped between Oskar and me. He put a shovel in Oskar's hand, pointed to a spot where the concrete of the sidewalk was torn up, exposing some earth, and ordered him to dig. A corpse was lying nearby.

While Oskar was digging, the Russian pulled me into the hallway of a half-destroyed building. Knowing what was coming, I used the strategy that had worked so well with my first attacker. Again I folded my arms around his neck. Again I clung to his body and, smiling, I repeated my welcome speech.

He was perplexed.

And then I tenderly whispered in his ear, "Oh, no. Not here. You come at night."

He stopped unbuttoning his trousers.

"My address," I said, "is Nollendorfplatz number ten. My name is Maria Shultz."

He picked up a scrap of singed paper from the ground, handed it to me, and said, "Write down."

I did. I caressed his cheek and said, "Bring vodka, will celebrate."

I wanted to leave, when another Russian arrived.

"You through?" he asked his comrade. "Now me."

He put a powerful arm around my waist, but he was pushed aside by the first Russian and forcefully pinned against the wall.

"This my German," the first Russian sputtered.

And I realized that I, with my calculated behavior, once more had succeeded in arousing a trace of chivalry in this wild, young soldier who now protected me.

Out in the street again, I had to stand by until the hole Oskar was shoveling was large enough to hold the corpse of a Russian soldier. This done, we were allowed to go on.

We were glad to find Karl's building still standing. It did not even show a scar. This was probably the reason it had now been chosen as a kind of Russian headquarters. Russians were milling around, singing, dancing, and stamping their feet.

In the entrance hall, they were dancing wildly around a gramophone which, at full volume, blasted the latest German hit song: *"Das ist ein Frühling ohne Ende,"* "This Is a Spring without an End."

So involved were they in their revelry that they neither saw nor stopped us. We went directly to the air-raid shelter, knowing Karl and his girl would not be in their apartment upstairs. Here, too, people had not left the shelter yet. It was dark and smelly.

We looked and called for Karl. Finally we found him, his head resting on arms tightly folded around his knees.

Hearing Oskar's voice, he looked up for a silent moment.

Could this really be Karl, I wondered. I had not met him before. But Oskar had often spoken about his friend, a painter who, though a deserter and living in steady danger, had never lost his positive and cheerful attitude toward life. I had also seen a portrait Oskar had painted of Karl just a few months ago: sparkling blue eyes in a roundish, smiling, and youthful face. Now his exhausted face was gray and pained, his eyes swollen and red-rimmed.

"Are you all right?" I asked, realizing the absurdity of my question.

"Where is Lotti?" Oskar asked.

"In a hospital—I hope," Karl muttered.

We did not dare to ask further questions. We waited. We waited for a long time until Karl, hesitantly, began to speak.

"They lined up in a row. About twenty of them. I fought hard, trying to hold back the first one who threw her on the mattress. I felt the cold metal of a pistol at my temple. Then my hands were bound behind my back. For more than an hour, soldier after soldier had his way with her. After the fifth or sixth, her screaming stopped. She closed her eyes, and I thought she was going to die. After the last of the rapists had gone, a new horde arrived, already unbuttoning their trousers. But an officer was at their heels. He looked at Lotti, looked at me, and harshly commanded the soldiers to leave. He ordered them to get an ambulance."

Karl fell silent.

"And then?" Oskar asked.

"The ambulance arrived surprisingly quickly. Lotti was carried away. But they didn't let me go with her."

Karl's head slumped down again. He was sobbing. Seldom had I felt so daunted in my life. There was nothing, absolutely nothing, one could do to help.

"Come with us," Oskar said.

But, of course, Karl didn't want to. He wanted to wait for Lotti's return. He also wanted to find out where she was.

"Do you have something to eat?" Oskar asked.

"The Russian officer said he would send some food from their kitchen."

For a while we stayed with Karl. We talked to him, but he did not seem to listen. Then he urged us to leave.

"Go now," he said and, with a smile of exasperation, he added: "Go and enjoy the breaking out of peace."

Disconcerted and depressed, we left.

"Where to now?" I asked.

"To my place," Oskar replied. "Let's see whether it still exists. But it will be a long and strenuous walk."

"I know," I said. "I'll manage."

However, just one block from where we were, there had once been a fine gallery, a bookstore on the ground floor with a stair leading to a small art gallery upstairs. We wanted to see whether it was still there.

It was. A single building in a row of ruins. We entered through an open door and found a raucous bivouac inside: a fire burning brightly in the center of the room. A fire! On the polished parquet floor in a room still nice and orderly! Russians squatted around the fire. Hanging from the tips of their gun barrels were chunks of meat, which they were roasting in the fire. Horse meat, I assumed.

A bottle made the rounds, was smashed against the wall when empty, and instantly replaced by a new one. When they noticed us, they seemed more amused than surprised and offered us the bottle. Each of us took a big slug, and we were coaxed to drink more. They even moved closer together and, gesturing, invited us to sit down, too.

We did. The warmth of the fire and the warmth of the vodka inside us did us good. It had been cold outdoors, a damp kind of coldness that got into your bones.

"It's all right," Oskar had said earlier. "The cold prevents the corpses from decaying too quickly."

One of the Russians got up. I squirmed and was afraid. Would he come to lay his hands on me? But he went straight to the wall lined with bookshelves, grabbed an armful of books, and threw them into the fire.

Oskar and I were aghast, but tried to hide it. Books don't burn as easily as one might think; they had to be poked with gun barrels to catch fire. Exuberant with childlike joy, the Russians poked and poked, sometimes stepping right into the flames. Since their uniforms were wet and crusted with dirt, they did not catch fire, either, which encouraged the soldiers to jump over the fire. Within minutes a witches' dance in and around the flames shook the floor under our feet.

Looking around, Oskar discovered chunks of meat stored in a corner. He showed them to me and said, "There must be sheets of paper around here somewhere. Go and look."

What does he want paper for? I wondered. I found some on a desk that must have held the cash register.

Oskar took a sheet and walked over to a soldier who, exhausted from dance and liquor, was leaning against a wall. In minutes Oskar drew a portrait of this young man that had a good likeness, although Oskar had drastically idealized his looks.

He showed it to the model, and the delight with which the young Russian looked at himself was touching.

Oskar reached out to take the picture away, but the soldier pressed it against his chest, shaking his head vigorously.

"Tell him," Oskar said to me, "he can keep it if he gives us some meat."

I did, and a bloody piece of meat was put into my hands. I wrapped it in a sheet of paper I snatched from the fire. It was a lovely reproduction of a Chagall painting.

Proudly the soldier showed his portrait to his comrades, and instantly Oskar was surrounded by the whole gang.

Pointing to themselves, they begged: "Me too picture! Me too!"

While Oskar drew, I went to the bookshelves and took two books. I did not feel like a thief or a plunderer. No. The books would have been thrown into the flames anyhow, and I felt rich with two volumes of Rilke in my blood-smeared hands.

And only at this moment, for the first time really, did I become aware that nothing belonged to me anymore. Nothing but what I had on my body. And a large bundle of German paper money, since I had sold many of my paintings during the last few months. Thinking of those paintings, a flicker of joy went through my mind: those paintings, which I had never signed with my real name because I was ashamed of them, those paintings, I hoped, would not have survived the battle of Berlin.

I went through my pocketbook to check on my possessions. The bundle of money took up a lot of space. I was tempted to throw it away, thinking it would have no value anymore. In addition, there was one handkerchief, the tiny box of cyanide capsules, a small sewing kit—how wise, I thought—and a clasp holding three keys to an apartment that did not exist anymore. That was all. But then, to my surprise, I felt something hard stuck in the folds of the lining.

I pulled it out and held a small golden heart in my hand. It was a locket I had worn on a golden chain around my neck when I was a child. It was one of those that could be opened to hold a photo on each side. What was in there? I had forgotten. Curious, I opened it and found on one side the dear face of my grandmother smiling at me. The other side was empty.

That was all I owned.

An hour passed. Oskar had sketched many portraits. After we were given more meat, we were ready to leave. There were endless thank-yous, saying *spasibo* back and forth. There were handshakes and embraces.

Now the long walk to Wilmersdorf, to Oskar's place, began. It was afternoon by now, and the situation in the streets had changed. Instead of the columns of captured German soldiers, we passed column after column of Russian vehicles: the Red Army support units, following the fighting troops. What a sight! Wagons drawn by horses or ponies. Soldiers, most of them, but also all kinds of camp followers, women among them. They sat on bales of hay, singing and guzzling. Many were dressed extravagantly: embroidered velvet capes, glittering blouses, even crowns on their heads. I, hardly trusting my eyes, felt as if I were watching a mad play or a wild masquerade procession.

And wagon after wagon followed, piled up with loot: not only bicycles, beds, carpets, and furniture, but also kitchen and bathroom sinks, even toilets. There were also live geese, ducks, chickens, and rabbits in cages. And hitched to the wagons were cows and goats.

Speechless we watched. Then we moved on. A few civilians were now in the streets with white kerchiefs round their arms and scarves over their faces to protect them against the soot and the stench in the air. Aimlessly they walked about.

Oskar urged me to quicken my pace. He wanted to reach his home, if it still stood, before dark. That, however, did not prevent him from stopping frequently to look at a corpse lying in our path.

While I averted my eyes, he studied it. When this happened the third time, I got angry and taunted him.

"Little sister," he said. "Little sister, this is part of life, too: death. Think of Leonardo da Vinci! He was interested in corpses. And he drew them well."

At moments like this, Oskar became an enigma to me. And I was not sure whether I liked him.

We walked in silence for quite some time until Oskar stepped in front of me and, with warmth and great concern, he asked, "How do you feel, little sister?"

"Fine," I lied. And we went on.

We came to the spot where, a few hours ago, the cadaver of the horse had been cut up by the starving people. All that was left now was the bare skeleton, a shred of hide hanging here and there.

Coming to the outer regions of Wilmersdorf, where smaller houses with small gardens in front of them stood, I became aware, painfully in a way, that it was spring. Long, bright yellow forsythia hedges, white daffodils, and even some early tulips were in bloom.

It was then that I saw a young German soldier across the street. He stood under an apple tree, densely covered with white blossoms. He seemed in a state of ecstasy with his arms raised above his head. Or . . . was he maybe in pain? I put my armful of books and meat on the ground and hurried across.

As soon as I was close, I saw he was dead. He leaned against the tree trunk. His head was raised and his brown eyes stared into the tent of blossoms above him.

"Rigor mortis," said Oskar matter-of-factly.

When a bird began to sing in the crown of the tree, it was too much for me. I burst into tears.

Oskar let me cry awhile before taking my hand and pulling me away.

And all of a sudden a mysterious change came over me: the horror subsided and allowed a calm I had not felt for many years to enter my senses. I once more looked into the brown eyes of the dead soldier. This time I thought I saw a faint smile on his face.

I tried to smile, too.

I turned to Oskar and said, "The war and the killing are over now."

"Yes," Oskar said, "Hitler is gone, and the twelve years of the Thousand Year Reich are over, too."

Chronology

· ——————————— ·

November 11, 1918   World War I ends. Hitler, though Austrian by birth, serves as a corporal in the Bavarian army. He emerges from the war an extreme nationalist, blaming Germany's defeat on the Jews and the Bolsheviks.

The Treaty of Versailles is signed, establishing the terms of the peace.

The constitution of the new Weimar Republic is approved.

1923–24   The Ruhr area of Germany is occupied by French and Belgian troops in response to Germany's failure to keep up her reparation payments under the terms of the Versailles Treaty.

With the help of the strongly nationalistic Socialist German Workers Party, Hitler attempts to seize the government of Bavaria: the so-called Beer Hall Putsch.

Post-war German inflation is now at its most extreme: 4.2 billion German marks equal one U.S. dollar.

After the "Putsch," Hitler is arrested and sentenced to Landberg Prison, where he serves nine months of a five-year sentence. Here he begins to write *Mein Kampf*, a compound of dreams of power, vicious anti-Semitic rantings, and a blueprint for conquering Europe.

1928   The Nazi Party (formerly the Socialist German Workers Party, now the National Socialist Party) receives 3 percent of the vote in general elections.

1930   In parliamentary elections, the National Socialist Party receives 18 percent of the vote. By 1929 the German economy had recovered, but the world economic depression soon followed, creating mass unemployment and countless business failures.

1932   Old Field Marshal von Hindenburg, Germany's soldier-hero, is re-elected president, defeating Hitler. However, Hitler, who has made promises to every segment of German society, receives 33 percent of the vote.

1933   Chaotic political and economic conditions follow, and an exhausted von Hindenburg appoints Hitler chancellor, hoping for stability.

In new elections, the Nazis win a majority, and the German parliament gives Hitler dictatorial powers.

Hitler has achieved power legally, but almost immediately hundreds of political opponents are jailed and/or executed.

All political parties except the Nazi Party are forced to disband, as are the trade unions.

Systematic boycotts of Jewish doctors, lawyers, and businessmen begin.

1934   With the death of von Hindenburg, the armed forces swear allegiance to Hitler.

1935   The anti-Semitic Nuremberg Laws are passed, depriving Jews of citizenship. Marriage between Jews and Germans is forbidden.

Military conscription becomes law.

1936   In violation of the Versailles Treaty, German troops enter and reoccupy the Rhineland. England and France acquiesce.

1938   Germany invades and annexes Austria.

Jews are forced to carry special passports in which they must carry the name of Israel or Sarah.

Crystal Night—Jews are attacked and their shops and offices vandalized. They are forbidden to visit German schools and other cultural institutions. Their driver's licenses are revoked and their movements severely restricted.

1939   The German army invades Czechoslovakia. The German-Russian peace treaty is signed.

Germany invades Poland in September, and World War II begins. Britain and France declare war on Germany.

1939–40   Deportation of Jews to Polish ghettos begins.

1940   Germany invades France and the Low Countries on May 10. On June 22, France falls to the Germans. The British evacuate their forces at Dunkirk.

1941   Germany invades Russia in violation of the German-Russian treaty.

Jews are forced to wear the yellow Star of David and are forbidden to emigrate. The property of deported Jews is seized.

Germany declares war on the United States.

1942   At Auschwitz the gassing of Jews begins.

1942–43   The battle of Stalingrad ends with a major defeat for the German army. The Allied armies invade Italy.

1944   On June 6, "D day," the Allied invasion of Europe begins. On July 20, a group of German army officers attempts, unsuccessfully, to assassinate Hitler and overthrow his regime. Mass executions of Jews follow.

1944–45   The Battle of the Bulge begins, and in March 1945 the Allied armies cross the Rhine.

1945   Hitler orders his "scorched earth policy" as the German armies retreat. The Russian army enters Austria at the end of March and advances toward Germany and Berlin. Although the war is clearly lost, Hitler commands all Germans to fight on to the death.

By the middle of April the battle of Berlin begins. On April 30, Hitler commits suicide.

On May 2, Berlin falls to the Russian forces. On May 7, Germany surrenders unconditionally.

Glossary

Abitur   The highest school certificate in the German educational system; it is roughly equivalent to junior standing at a U.S. college and is a prerequisite for university study.

B.D.M.   *Bund Deutscher Mädchen*, literally League of German Maidens (young girls). Female equivalent to the Hitler *Jugend* (Hitler Youth), which was for boys only.

Deutschlandsender   The main German radio station in Königswusterhausen, close to Berlin, which, like all sources of information, was taken over by the Nazis. In addition to regular broadcasts (entertainment, sports, news, and propaganda), it always gave detailed information and warnings on the approach of Allied bombers.

Gestapo   Abbreviation for *Geheime Staatspolizei*, Secret State Police, whose branches reached throughout Germany and occupied Europe.

Golden Party Badge   Sign of a longtime member or one who had performed unusual services for the Party.

Götterdämmerung   In Germanic mythology, this is the end of the world; the time when the gods war with their enemies until all are destroyed. It is also the title for the fourth and last opera of the tetralogy of *Der Ring Der (oder Des) Nibelungen* (The Ring of the Nibelung) by Richard Wagner.

Mother Cross   Women who had given birth to more than five children were decorated with the Mother Cross.

Horst Wessel Lied   The official song of the Nazi Party.

Jewishness   The orthodox Jewish religion declares a person who has a Jewish mother (not father) to be a Jew. The fact that the mother might be married to an Aryan does not make the offspring half Jewish; this term does not exist in Judaism. Hitler's laws, however, declared a person who had a Jewish father or Jewish mother married to an Aryan to be a *Mischling*, literally a mixed one. A child with one Jewish parent was a Mischling first degree. Having a Jewish grandfather or grandmother made the grandchild a Mischling second degree, and so on.

Oberkommando der Wehrmacht Supreme Command of the German Armed Forces.

One-Pot-Day Once a week every restaurant had to serve nothing but a one-pot meal.

S.A. Abbreviation for *Sturm Abteilung*, literally Storm Detachment. Originally designed as a private army of the Nazi Party to protect Nazi meetings and to fight political adversaries. Their uniform was brown, in contrast to the black uniform of the S.S.

S.S. Abbreviation for *Schutz Staffel*, literally Protection Squad. Originally consisting of only twenty-six men to be Hitler's personal bodyguard. Heinrich Himmler transformed the S.S. later into a mass army and powerful administration, penetrating into every sector of German society, down to the guards of the concentration camps. Tall, blond, and blue-eyed, they were considered to be the Aryan elite. Their uniform was black.

Sarah and Israel In August 1938 a special passport was introduced in which every Jew was compelled to carry the name Israel (for a male) or Sarah (for a female) in his or her passport.

Star of David In September 1941 a regulation was issued: Every Jew had to wear the yellow Star of David on his or her sleeve.

Volkssturm A military Home Guard, hastily organized toward the end of the war, consisting of veterans of World War I and boys who had not yet reached military age. Hitler's decree in October 1944 demanded that all men between sixteen and sixty who were capable of bearing arms be drafted.

Wehrmacht Armed Forces

Weltanschauung Literally a way of looking at the world; a conception of the world. But it encompasses more: the philosophical, religious, political, and pragmatic attitude toward life and death—toward the whole world.

Wunderwaffe Literally the wonder weapon. It was a very early type of missile capable of great destruction.

Personae

Rudolph König
Dead

Fred
Real name is Herberth Kiehne. Last heard of during the eighties, when
he alternated his living quarters between Morocco and Spain.
Sickly then, he may no longer be living.

Vera
Missing since 1944 without any trace

Otto
Missing since 1945 without any trace

Hajo
Not seen nor heard of since September 1945. Rumored
to have left West Berlin for East Germany and Poland.

Oskar
I saw him last in 1986 in a bar in West Berlin, which served
as his address at that time. A letter, sent later to the bar,
was returned as undeliverable. Other efforts to locate him were
unsuccessful. Then, while visiting Berlin in 1992, I learned
of his death in September 1991.

Christa, Anna, Theo, and Sven
No contact with nor knowledge of for almost fifty years